P9-DNN-484

Better Homes and Gardens.

Forever Favorite
CROCHET

◆ ◆ ◆

© Copyright 1984 by Meredith Corporation, Des Moines, Iowa.
All Rights Reserved. Printed in the United States of America.
First Edition. Fifth Printing, 1986.
Library of Congress Catalog Card Number: 83-63302
ISBN: 0-696-01195-6 (hard cover)
ISBN: 0-696-01197-2 (trade paperback)

BETTER HOMES AND GARDENS® BOOKS

Editor: Gerald M. Knox
Art Director: Ernest Shelton
Managing Editor: David A. Kirchner

Crafts Editor: Nancy Lindemeyer
Senior Crafts Books Editor: Joan Cravens
Associate Crafts Books Editors: Debra Felton,
    Laura Holtorf, Rebecca Jerdee, Sara Jane Treinen

Associate Art Directors: Linda Ford Vermie,
    Neoma Alt West, Randall Yontz
Copy and Production Editors: Marsha Jahns,
    Mary Helen Schiltz, Carl Voss, David A. Walsh
Assistant Art Directors: Harijs Priekulis,
    Tom Wegner
Senior Graphic Designers: Alisann Dixon,
    Lynda Haupert, Lyne Neymeyer
Graphic Designers: Mike Burns, Mike Eagleton,
    Deb Miner, Stan Sams, D. Greg Thompson,
    Darla Whipple, Paul Zimmerman

Vice President, Editorial Director: Doris Eby
Executive Director, Editorial Services: Duane L. Gregg

General Manager: Fred Stines
Director of Publishing: Robert B. Nelson
Vice President, Retail Marketing: Jamie Martin
Vice President, Direct Marketing: Arthur Heydendael

Forever Favorite Crochet
Crafts Editors: Joan Cravens, Sara Jane Treinen
Copy and Production Editor: Marsha Jahns
Graphic Designer: Alisann Dixon
Electronic Text Processor: Donna Russell

Contents

PLEASURES TO STITCH—ELEGANT DOILIES 4

Even a beginner can crochet a doily, and
the three spectacular designs here prove
the point. Look in this section also for floral
motifs to delight even the most experienced stitcher.

BEST-LOVED EDGINGS FOR A PERSONAL TOUCH 16

Creating one-of-a-kind linens and accessories
for your home or family is easy with crocheted
edgings. Stitch any or all of these designs
using a variety of threads and yarns, then
use them to personalize place mats, bed linens,
scarves, skirts, and more.

CROCHETING PRIMER 24

Learn to crochet or improve your skills with
this review of hooks, yarns, and stitchery tips,
plus abbreviations and stitch diagrams.

LACY ACCENTS FOR YOUR HOME 28

What more beautiful way is there to dress up your
house than with handmade lace. Here are
elegant pillows, a table runner, curtains, a tablecloth,
and bedspreads to make and cherish for years to come.

WARM, COZY SWEATERS FOR ALL THE FAMILY 46

These crocheted cardigans, pullovers, and jackets
are suitable for every season and for men,
women, and children as well.

FAVORITE DESIGNS FOR AFGHANS AND PILLOWS 62

Need a finishing touch for a favorite room
or a special gift for a friend? One of these ten
designs is sure to fill the bill.

ACKNOWLEDGMENTS 80

ELEGANT DOILIES

Displaying all the color and charm
of a country garden, these doilies will add
just the right finishing touch—decorative
and personal—to your home. In the
remaining sections of this book, you'll
find an equally delightful array of edgings,
afghans, lacy accessories, and classic
sweaters to crochet, plus professional tips to
help you perfect your stitching technique.

Graceful leaves, pansies and roses,
all favorite motifs in Irish crochet, adorn
most of these doilies. Shown at *left
front* is a doily with blue flowers; behind it is
one with a pansy border. The ruffle-edge
doily, to the *right,* is worked in variegated
pastel thread. Simple pink roses and
green leaves border the doily at *center front;*
fuller roses bloom amid the leaves on
the yellow doily, *center back.* At *right front*
is a five-sided doily, with flowers in
two sizes. Instructions begin on page 8.

ELEGANT DOILIES

♦ ♦ ♦

Even a novice crochet-er can stitch spectac-ular doilies by start-ing with one of the projects pictured here. Chain, single, and double crochet are the only stitches you need to master to make the large pine-apple pattern doily, *opposite,* the center-piece doily (with vio-lets), *above,* and the five-sided pineapple doily, *right.*

Crocheted with the threads recommend-ed in the instructions, these designs mea-sure between 21 and 28 inches in diameter.

Doily with Blue Flowers
Shown on page 4

Finished size is approximately 14½ inches in diameter.

MATERIALS
- Coats & Clark Knit-Cro-Sheen (50-yard balls), Size 5: 1 ball each of green and yellow; 2 balls each of blue and white
- Size 9 steel crochet hook

Abbreviations: See pages 26-27.

INSTRUCTIONS
With white ch 8; sl st to form ring.

Rnd 1: Ch 3, work 24 dc in ring, sl st to top of beg ch-3.

Rnd 2: * Ch 5, sk 1 dc, sc in next dc. Rep from * 11 times more. *Note:* Do not join rnds.

Rnd 3: * Ch 6, sc in ch-5 lp made in Rnd 2. Rep from * 11 times more.

Rnd 4: * Ch 7, sc in ch-6 lp made in Rnd 3. Rep from * 11 times more.

Rnd 5: Ch 1, * in next ch-7 lp work **3 dc, ch 3, 3 dc—shell made;** ch 4. Rep from * 11 times more.

Rnd 6: * In next ch-3 sp work shell, ch 5. Rep from * 11 times more.

Rnds 7-13: Work same as for Rnd 6, except increase number of chains by 1 between shells on each rnd: Rnd 7, ch 6; Rnd 8, ch 7; Rnd 9, ch 8; Rnd 10, ch 9; Rnd 11, ch 10; Rnd 12, ch 11; Rnd 13, ch 12.

End with shell on last rep.

Note: Rnds 13-17 end with shells.

Rnd 14: * Ch 8, sc in ch-12 lp, ch 8, shell in next ch-3 sp. Rep from * around.

Rnd 15: * Ch 9, trc in sc, ch 9, shell in next ch-3 sp. Rep from * around.

Rnd 16: * Ch 10, sc in trc, ch 10, shell in ch-3 sp. Rep from * around.

Rnd 17: * Ch 18, skip next 2 ch-10 lps, dc in next 3 dc, 7 dc in ch-3 sp of shell, dc in next 3 dc. Rep from * around.

Rnd 18: Ch 8, * sc in ch-18 lp, ch 8, work (trc, ch 1) in each dc of shell—13 trc made; ch 8. Rep from *, ending with 13th trc (omit ch-1).

Rnd 19: * Ch 8, skip next 2 ch-8 lps, (trc in next trc, ch 2) 12 times; trc in last trc. Rep from * around.

Rnd 20: * Ch 6, sc in first trc, (4 sc in ch-2 sp, sk trc) 12 times. Rep from * around, ending with 4 sc bet last 2 trc on rnd.

Rnd 21: Sk trc, sl st in first 3 ch of ch-6 from Rnd 20, * ch 3, sk 4 sc, trc in next sc; (ch 3, sk 3 sc, trc in next sc) 10 times; ch 3, sc in ch-6. Rep from * around, ending with trc, ch 3. *Rnd 22:* Sc in third sl st made at beg of Rnd 21, work 3 sc in next ch-3 sp, * in each of next 10 ch-3 sps work (**sc, hdc, dc, hdc, sc**)—**scallop made;** 3 sc in each of next 2 ch-3 sps. Rep from * around, ending with 3 sc in last sp.

Rnd 23: Sl st in next 5 sts, sc in next dc (top of scallop); * ch 15, sk 2 scallops, sc in top of next scallop. Rep from * around; (sps with 3 sc count as scallop). End with ch 15, sl st to first sc.

Rnd 24: Sl st in each of next 8 ch of ch-15 lp, ch 3, work a **2-trc-cl in same sp as follows: * yo hook twice, draw up loop in same sp, (yo, draw through 2 loops on hook) twice; repeat from * one more time; yo, draw through rem 3 lps on hook. ** Ch 11, work a 3-trc-cl in next sp as follows: [yo hook twice, draw up loop in sp, (yo, draw through 2 lps on hook) twice] 3 times; draw through rem 4 lps on hook.** Rep from ** around; end with ch 11, join with sl st to top of 2-trc-cl. Fasten off.

Stem and leaves: With right side of doily facing, attach green on lp made in Rnd 4 bet 2 grps of 3 dc, * ch 3, sc in ch-3 sp bet 2 grps of 3 dc directly above in next rnd. Rep from * outward toward edge 8 times more. Work 11 more stems around doily in same manner. Fasten off each time.

Leaf: Ch 10, attach with sl st to the eighth st of ch-12 in Rnd 13 on right side of stem. Sc in second ch from hook, hdc in next ch, dc in next 5 chs, hdc in next ch, sc in last ch, sl st to last sc in stem.

Rep leaf as before except attach in third st of ch-12 in Rnd 13 on the left side of stem, ch 1, turn, continue as before. Rep leaf again except attach to left in third st of ch-9 in Rnd 15 on the left side of stem, ch 1, turn, continue as before. End with sl st to last sc of stem, sl st in ch-3 sp of next shell above. Fasten off. Rep for each line of shells—12 stems. (*Note:* Wrong side of leaf will appear faceup.)

Flowers (make 12): With yellow, ch 6, sl st to form ring.

Rnd 1: * Ch 6, sc in second ch from hook and in next 4 sts, sc in ring. Rep from * 5 times more—6 petals formed. Fasten off.

Rnd 2: Attach blue in ring, work 2 sc in ring bet each petal. Hold petals forward and keep them unattached. (*Note:* Do not join rnds.)

Rnd 3: Work 2 sc in each sc around; in last st work 3 sc—25 sc; ch 1. *Rnd 4:* (Work dc in each of next 5 sc, ch 1) 5 times; join with sl st to ch-1 at beg of rnd.

Rnd 5: * In first dc of 5-dc grp work hdc and dc; 2 dc in next dc, 3 trc in next dc, 2 dc in next dc, dc and hdc in last dc, sl st in ch-1 sp. Rep from * 4 times—5 petals; sl st to ch-1. Fasten off.

Sew flowers to doily, matching flower center with hole formed by 7 dc in ch-3 sp of Rnd 17. Align flowers with stem and leaves.

Doily with Pansy Border
Shown on page 4

Finished doily is about 9½ inches in diameter.

MATERIALS
- Clark's Big Ball mercerized cotton, Size 30: 1 ball of white and a small amount of the same size thread in various colors for 19 pansies
- Size 10 steel crochet hook

INSTRUCTIONS

With white, ch 8; join with sl st to form ring.

Rnd 1: Ch 3, make 18 dc in ring; join to top of ch-3—19 dc, counting ch-3 as 1 dc.

Rnd 2: Ch 4, * dc in back lp of next dc, ch 1. Rep from * around; join to third ch of ch-4—19 sps.

Rnd 3: Ch 5, * dc in next dc, ch 2. Rep from * around; join to third ch of ch-5.

Rnd 4: Ch 3, dc in joining, ch 2, * 2 dc in next dc, ch 2. Rep from * around; join to top of ch-3—19 spokes started.

Rnd 5: Ch 3, 2 dc in next dc, ch 2, * dc in next dc, 2 dc in next dc, ch 2. Rep from * around; join as before.

Rnd 6: Ch 3, dc in next dc, 2 dc in next dc, ch 2, * dc in next 2 dc, 2 dc in next dc, ch 2. Rep from * around; join.

Rnd 7-9: Ch 3, * dc in each dc to within 1 dc before next ch-2 sp, 2 dc in next dc, ch 2. Rep from * around; join.

Rnd 10: Ch 3, * dc in each dc to next ch-2 sp, ch 2. Rep from * around; join.

Rnd 11: Ch 3, * dc in each dc to within 1 dc before next ch-2 sp, ch 1, dc in next dc, ch 2. Rep from * around; join.

Rnd 12: Ch 3, dc in next 4 dc, (ch 1, dc in next dc) twice; ch 2, * dc in next 5 dc, (ch 1, dc in next dc) twice; ch 2. Rep from * around; join.

Rnd 13: Ch 3, dc in next 3 dc, (ch 1, dc in next dc) 3 times; ch 2, * dc in next 4 dc, (ch 1, dc in next dc) 3 times; ch 2. Rep from * around; join.

Rnd 14: Ch 3, dc in next 2 dc, (ch 1, dc in next dc) 4 times; ch 2, * dc in next 3 dc, (ch 1, dc in next dc) 4 times; ch 2. Rep from * around; join.

Rnd 15: Ch 3, dc in next dc, (ch 1, dc in next dc) 5 times; ch 2, * dc in next 2 dc, (ch 1, dc in next dc) 5 times; ch 2. Rep from * around; join.

Rnd 16: Ch 6, sk next 2 dc, sc in next dc, * ch 3; in next ch-2 sp make **3 dc, ch 2, 3 dc—open shell made;** ch 3, sk next 3 dc, sc in next dc. Rep from * around, ending with 3 dc, ch 2 and 2 dc in last ch-2 sp. Join to third ch of ch-6. Fasten off.

Pansy (make 19): Beg at center with any color, ch 10; join with sl st to form ring.

Rnd 1: Ch 3, 4 dc in ring, (ch 2, 5 dc in ring) 4 times; ch 2; join to top of ch-3.

Rnd 2 (right side of pansy): Sl st in next dc, ch 1, sc in following dc, (ch 1, in next ch-2 sp make **4 dc, ch 1, 4 dc—4-dc shell made;** ch 1, sk 2 dc, sc in next dc) 3 times; mark last shell worked; ch 1, (10 trc in next ch-2 sp) twice; ch 1. Join to first sc; ch 4, turn.

Next row: (Dc in next trc, ch 1) 20 times; sc in next dc; turn.

Following row: Sl st in first sp and in next dc, ch 1, sc in next sp, (ch 3, sc in next sp) 18 times, sl st in next dc. Fasten off.

Joining rnd: Using color of your choice, work as follows: With right side of doily facing, join thread to sc bet 2 open shells of Rnd 16, ch 1, sc in same sc, * ch 5, with right side of pansy facing, sc in ch-1 sp of marked shell on a pansy, ch 5, sc in ch-2 sp of next shell on center of doily, (sl st in ch-1 sp of next shell on same pansy, ch 5) twice; sc in next sc on center. Rep from * until all pansies have been joined to center. Fasten off.

Variegated Doily
Shown on page 4

Finished doily measures 12 inches in diameter.

MATERIALS
- Clark's Big Ball mercerized cotton, Size 30: 1 variegated ball each of blue, pink, yellow, and green
- Size 11 steel crochet hook

INSTRUCTIONS
Beg at center with yellows, ch 6; join with sl st to form ring.

Rnd 1: Ch 3, make 23 dc in ring; join to top of ch-3—24 dc, counting ch-3 as 1 dc.

Rnd 2: Ch 3; * **2 dc in next dc—inc made;** dc in next dc. Rep from * around, ending with 2 dc in last dc; join as before—36 dc.

Rnds 3-4: Ch 3, inc 12 dc evenly spaced, dc in each dc around; join—60 dc on Rnd 4. Fasten off yellows; join pinks to top of ch-3.

Rnds 5-6: Work as for Rnd 3—84 dc on Rnd 6. Fasten off pinks; join greens to top of ch-3.

Rnd 7: Ch 3, dc in next dc, * 2 dc in next dc, dc in next 2 dc. Rep from * around, ending with 2 dc in last dc; join—112 dc.

Rnd 8: Ch 3, * 2 dc in next dc, dc in next 7 dc. Rep from * around, ending with dc in last 6 dc; join—126 dc.

Rnd 9: Ch 3, * 2 dc in next dc, dc in next 13 dc. Rep from * around, ending with dc in last 12 dc; join—135 dc. Fasten off greens; join pinks to top of ch-3.

Rnd 10: Ch 3, dc in next 4 dc, * 2 dc in next dc, dc in next 12 dc. Rep from * around; join—145 dc.

Rnd 11: Ch 3, 2 dc in next dc, * dc in next 9 dc, 2 dc in next dc. Rep from * around, ending with dc in last 3 dc; join—160 dc. Fasten off pinks; join yellows to top of ch-3.

Rnd 12: Ch 3, dc in next 2 dc, ch 3, sk 2 dc, * dc in next 3 dc, ch 3, sk 2 dc. Rep from * around; join—32 sps.

Rnd 13: Sl st in next 2 dc and in next sp, **ch 3, in same sp make dc, ch 2, and 2 dc—beg shell made;** ch 1; * in next ch-3 sp make **2 dc, ch 2, and 2 dc—shell made;** ch 1. Rep from * around; join—32 shells.

Rnds 14-16: Sl st in next dc and in next sp, make beg shell in same sp, ch 1; * shell in sp of next shell, ch 1. Rep from * around; join. Fasten off yellows; join greens to any ch-2 sp. *Rnd 17:* Ch 1, sc in same sp, * ch 5, sc in next ch-1 sp, ch 5, sc in sp of next shell. Rep from * around, ending with ch-2, dc in first sc to form last lp—64 lps.

Rnds 18-20: Ch 1, sc in lp just formed, * ch 5, sc in next lp. Rep from * around, ending with ch 2, dc in first sc.

continued

Rnd 21: Ch 4, make 2 trc in same lp, ch 3, * 3 trc in next lp, ch 3. Rep from * around; join to top of ch-4.

Rnd 22: Sl st in next 2 trc and in next sp, ch 4, in same sp make **trc, ch 2, and 2 trc—beg trc-shell made;** * in next sp make **2 trc, ch 2, and 2 trc—trc-shell made.** Rep from * around; join to top of ch-4.

Rnd 23: Sl st in next trc and in next sp, ch 4 and complete beg trc-shell; * trc-shell over next trc-shell. Rep from * around; join.

Rnd 24: Making ch-1 bet each shell, work as for Rnd 22—64 shells. Fasten off pinks; join blues to any shell sp.

Rnd 25: Rep Rnd 17—128 lps.

Rnds 26-28: Rep Rnd 18.

Rnd 29: Rep Rnd 21. Fasten off blues; join pinks to any ch-3 sp.

Rnds 30-31: Work as for Rnds 22 and 24.

Rnd 32: Work as for Rnd 17; join—256 lps. Fasten off pinks; join greens to any lp.

Rnd 33: Ch 1, sc in same lp, * ch 7, sk next lp; make 4 trc in next lp, ch 3, sc in top of last trc made, make 4 trc in same lp; ch 7, sk next lp, sc in next lp. Rep from * around, ending with ch-7; join to first sc. Fasten off.

Doily with Leaves and Pink Roses
Shown on page 4

Finished size of doily is about 12 inches in diameter.

—————— **MATERIALS** ——————
• J. & P. Coats Knit-Cro-Sheen: 1 ball each of white, variegated pink, green, and a few yards of yellow
• Size 8 steel crochet hook

Abbreviations: See pages 26-27.

—————— **INSTRUCTIONS** ——————
Beg at center with white, ch 8; join with sl st to form ring.

Rnd 1: Ch 1, make 10 sc in ring; join to first sc.

Rnd 2: **Ch 3, holding back on hook last lp of each dc make 2 dc in joining, thread over and draw through all lps on hook— beg cluster made;** ch 2; * **holding back on hook last lp of each dc make 3 dc in next sc, thread over and draw through all lps on hook—cluster (cl) made;** ch 2. Rep from * around; join to top of beg cl.

Rnd 3: Ch 1, sc in joining, * ch 3, sc in next ch-2 sp, ch 3, sc in tip of next cl. Rep from * around, ending with ch 3, sc in last ch-2 sp, ch 1, hdc in first sc to form last lp—20 lps. *Rnd 4:* Ch 1, sc in lp just formed, * ch 3, sc in next lp. Rep from * around, ending with ch 1, hdc in first sc to form last lp.

Rnd 5: Make a beg cl in lp just formed, * ch 3, sc in next lp, ch 3, cl in next lp. Rep from * around, ending with ch 3, sc in last lp, ch 1, hdc in top of beg cl.

Rnd 6: Rep Rnd 4.

Rnd 7: Beg cl in lp just formed, * ch 4, 2 sc in next lp, ch 4, cl in next lp. Rep from * around, ending with ch 1, dc in top of beg cl.

Rnd 8: Ch 1, 2 sc in lp just formed, * ch 5, 2 sc in next lp. Rep from * around, ending with ch 2, dc in first sc.

Rnd 9: Ch 1, 2 sc in same lp, * ch 6, cl in next lp, ch 6, 2 sc in next lp. Rep from * around, ending with ch 3, dc in first sc.

Rnd 10: Ch 1, 2 sc in same lp, * ch 7, 2 sc in next lp. Rep from * around, ending with ch 3, trc in first sc.

Rnd 11: Ch 1, 2 sc in same lp, * ch 8, cl in next lp, ch 8, 2 sc in next lp. Rep from * around, ending with ch 4, trc in first sc.

Rnd 12: Ch 1, 2 sc in same lp, * ch 9, 2 sc in next lp. Rep from * around, ending with ch 9; join to first sc.

Rnd 13: Sl st in next sc and first 2 ch of first lp; in same lp make beg cl, ch 8 and cl; ch 1; * in next lp make cl, ch 8, and cl; ch 1. Rep from * around; join to first cl. Fasten off.

Rose (make 10): Beg at center, with yellow, ch 4; join with sl st to form ring.

Rnd 1: Ch 6, (dc in ring, ch 3) 5 times; join to third ch of beg ch-6. Fasten off yellow.

Rnd 2: Join pink in any ch-3 sp, ch 1; in each sp around make (sc, hdc, 3 dc, hdc, and sc); join to first sc—6 petals.

Rnd 3: Ch 1, sc in joining, ch 5, * sc in sp bet last sc on next petal and first sc on following petal, ch 5. Rep from * around; join to first sc. *Note:* Keep ch-5 lps behind petals.

Rnd 4: Ch 1; in each ch-5 lp around make (sc, hdc, 5 dc, hdc, and sc); join to first sc.

Rnd 5: Ch 1, sc in joining, ch 7, * sc in sp bet last sc on next petal and first sc on following petal, ch 7. Rep from * around; join to first sc.

Rnd 6: Ch 1; in each ch-7 lp around make (sc, hdc, dc, 4 trc, dc, hdc, and sc); join. Fasten off.

Leaf (make 10): Beg at tip, with green, ch 13. *Row 1:* Sc in second ch from hook and in next 10 ch, 3 sc in last ch; working along opposite side of beg ch, sc in next 9 ch; ch 1, turn.

Note: Hereafter, work in back lp only of each sc.

Row 2: Sc in each sc to within center sc of the 3-sc grp; in center sc make sc, ch 1, and sc; sc in each sc to within last 2 sc—do not work in last 2 sc; ch 1, turn.

Row 3: Sc in each sc to within the ch-1 sp; in ch-1 sp make sc, ch 1, and sc; sc in each sc to within last 2 sc; ch 1, turn.

Rows 4-10: Work as for Row 3.

Row 11: Sc in each sc to within the ch-1 sp; in ch-1 sp make sc, ch 1, and sc; sc in each sc across. Fasten off. Now join the 10 roses to white center as follows:

Joining rnd: Join green to any ch-1 sp on last rnd of white center, ch 1, sc in same place, * ch 5, cl in next ch-8 lp on center, sc in center of any petal on last rnd of a rose, make cl in same ch-8 lp on center, ch 5, sc in next ch-1 sp on center, ch

5, cl in next ch-8 lp on center, sc in center of next petal on same rose, cl in same ch-8 lp on center, ch 5, sc in next ch-1 sp on center. Rep from * around, ending with ch 5; join to first sc. Fasten off.

Place a leaf bet 2 roses; tack to center sts of rose petals.

Yellow Doily with Roses
Shown on page 4

Doily is 16 inches in diameter.

──────MATERIALS──────
- J. & P. Coats Knit-Cro-Sheen: 1 ball each of variegated yellow, variegated pink, hunter green
- Size 7 steel crochet hook

Abbreviations: See pages 26-27.

─────── INSTRUCTIONS ───────
Beg at center, with yellow, ch 10; join with sl st to form ring.

Rnd 1: Ch 3, make 31 dc in ring; join to top of beg ch-3—32 dc, counting ch-3 as 1 dc.

Rnd 2: Ch 3, 2 dc in next dc, * dc in next dc, 2 dc in next dc. Rep from * around; join to top of beg ch-3—48 dc, counting ch-3 as 1 dc.

Rnd 3: Ch 1, sc in joining, * ch 11, sk next dc, sc in next dc. Rep from * around, ending with ch 5, triple treble crochet (tr trc—yo 3 times, draw through 2 lps on hook 4 times) in first sc to form last lp—24 lps.

Rnds 4-8: Ch 1, sc in lp just formed, * ch 11, sc in next lp. Rep from * around, ending with ch 5, tr trc in first sc.

Rnd 9: **Ch 3, in same lp make dc, ch 3, and 2 dc—beg shell made;** ch 3; * in next lp make **2 dc, ch 3, and 2 dc—shell made;** ch 3. Rep from * around; join to top of beg ch-3.

Rnd 10: Sl st in next dc and in next sp; **ch 3, in same sp make 3 dc, ch 3, and 4 dc—beg large shell made;** sc in next ch-3 sp bet shells; * in sp of next shell **make 4 dc, ch 3, and 4 dc—large shell made;** sc in next ch-3 sp bet shells. Rep from * around; join to top of ch-3 at beg of rnd; fasten off.

First rose: Beg at center with pinks, ch 6; join with sl st to form ring.

Rnd 1: Ch 1, 12 sc in ring; join to first sc.

Rnd 2: Ch 1, sc in joining, * ch 3, sk 1 sc, sc in next sc. Rep from * around; join with sl st to first sc.

Rnd 3: In each lp around make sc, hdc, 3 dc, hdc, and sc; join.

Rnd 4: * Ch 4, sc in back of work in sc bet this and next petal. Rep from * around; join.

Rnd 5: In each lp around make sc, hdc, 5 dc, hdc, and sc; join.

Rnd 6: * Ch 5, sc in back of work in sc bet this and next petal. Rep from * around; join.

Rnd 7: In each lp around make sc, hdc, 7 dc, hdc, and sc; join.

Rnd 8: * Ch 6, sc in back of work in sc bet this and next petal. Rep from * around; join.

Rnd 9: In each lp around make sc, hdc, 9 dc, hdc, and sc; join.

Rnd 10: * Ch 7, sc in back of work in sc bet this and next petal. Rep from * around; join.

Rnd 11: Make sc, hdc, and 5 dc in first lp, sl st in ch-3 sp of any shell of last rnd on center; in same lp of rose make 6 dc, hdc, and sc; in next lp on rose make sc, hdc, and 5 dc, sl st in ch-3 of next shell on Center; in same lp on rose make 6 dc, hdc, and sc; (in next lp on rose sc, hdc, 11 dc, hdc, and sc) 4 times; join. Fasten off.

Second rose: With the yellow, work same as for first rose until Rnd 10 has been completed.

Rnd 11: Make sc, hdc, and 5 dc in first lp, sl st in ch-3 sp of next shell on center to the left of previous joined rose; in same lp on rose make 6 dc, hdc, and sc; in next lp on rose make sc, hdc, and 5 dc, sl st in ch-3 of next shell on center; in same lp on rose make 6 dc, hdc, and sc; (in next lp on rose make sc, hdc, 11 dc, hdc, and sc) 3 times; in next lp make sc, hdc, 5 dc, sl st in dc of corresponding petal on previous rose; in same lp on rose in progress make 6 dc, hdc, and sc; join. Fasten off—second rose joined to first.

Alternating pinks and yellows for roses, work as for second rose, joining petals of last rose to corresponding petals of adjacent roses.

Leaf (make 12): Beg at tip with green, ch 15.

Row 1: Sc in second ch from hook, sc in each ch to within last ch, 3 sc in last ch, mark center st for tip of leaf; sc in each ch along opposite side of beg ch, sc in same place as last sc. Mark last sc for base of leaf. Hereafter, pick up only the back lp of each sc. Do not turn, but work sc in each sc to within 1 sc from center sc at tip of leaf; ch 1, turn.

Row 2: Sc in each sc to marked sc, 3 sc in marked sc, sc in each sc on other side to within 1 sc from center sc at tip of leaf; ch 1, turn.

Rows 3-10: Sc in each sc to within center sc of 3-sc grp, 3 sc in next sc, sc in each sc on other side to within last sc; ch 1, turn. At end of last row, fasten off.

Place a leaf bet each of 2 roses and tack in place.

Five-Sided Green Doily
Shown on page 5

Finished size of doily is about 13½ inches in diameter.

──────MATERIALS──────
- Clark's Big Ball mercerized cotton, Size 30: 1 ball main color (MC), 1 ball each of colors of your choice (colors A and B)
- Size 11 steel crochet hook

Abbreviations: See pages 26-27.

─────── INSTRUCTIONS ───────
Beg at center with MC, ch 8; join with sl st to form ring. *Rnd 1:* Ch 3, 19 dc in ring; join to top of ch-3.

Rnd 2: Ch 4, trc in same place as sl st, * sk next dc, 5 trc in next dc, sk next dc, 2 trc in next dc. Rep from * around; join to top of ch-4.

continued

11

Rnd 3: Ch 4, trc in same place as sl st, * ch 2, trc in next 2 trc, 5 trc in next trc, trc in next 2 trc, ch 2, trc in next 2 trc. Rep from * around; join as before.

Rnd 4: Ch 3, dc in next trc, * ch 4, sc in next trc, ch 3, sk next 2 trc, trc in next trc, 5 trc in next trc, trc in next trc, ch 3, sk next 2 trc, sc in next trc, ch 4, dc in next 2 trc. Rep from * around; join to top of ch-3.

Rnd 5: Ch 3, dc in next dc, * ch 4, sc in next sp, ch 4, trc in next 3 trc, 5 trc in next trc, trc in next 3 trc, ch 4, sk next sp, sc in next sp, ch 4, dc in next 2 dc. Rep from * around; join to top of ch-3.

Rnd 6: Ch 3, dc in next dc, * ch 4, sc in next sp, ch 5, trc in next trc, ch 2, sk next 2 trc, trc in next 2 trc, 5 trc in next trc, trc in next 2 trc, ch 2, sk next 2 trc, trc in next trc, ch 5, sk next sp, sc in next sp, ch 4, dc in next 2 dc. Rep from * around; join as before.

Rnd 7: Ch 3, dc in next dc, * ch 4, sc in next sp, ch 5, trc in next trc, ch 3, trc in next 4 trc, 5 trc in next trc, trc in next 4 trc, ch 3, trc in next trc, ch 5, sk next sp, sc in next sp, ch 4, dc in next 2 dc. Rep from * around; join as before.

Rnd 8: Ch 3, dc in next dc, * ch 4, sc in next sp, ch 5, trc in next trc, ch 3, trc in next trc, ch 3, sk next 2 trc, trc in next 3 trc, 5 trc in next trc, trc in next 3 trc, ch 3, sk next 2 trc, trc in next trc, ch 3, trc in next trc, ch 5, sk next sp, sc in next sp, ch 4, dc in next 2 dc. Rep from * around; join as before.

Rnd 9: Ch 3, dc in next dc, * ch 4, sc in next sp, ch 5 (trc in next trc, ch 3) twice; trc in next 5 trc, 5 trc in next trc, trc in next 5 trc, (ch 3, trc in next trc) twice; ch 5, sk next sp, sc in next sp, ch 4, dc in next 2 dc. Rep from * around; join as before.

Rnd 10: Ch 3, dc in next dc, * ch 4, sc in next sp, ch 5, (trc in next trc, ch 3) 3 times; sk next 2 trc, trc in next 4 trc, 5 trc in next trc, trc in

next 4 trc, ch 3, sk next 2 trc, (trc in next trc, ch 3) twice; ch 5, sk next sp, sc in next sp, ch 4, dc in next 2 dc. Rep from * around; join as before. Fasten off.

Flower motif: Beg at center with B, ch 8; join with sl st to form ring. *Rnd 1:* Ch 3, 19 dc in ring; join to top of beg ch-3.

Rnd 2: Ch 1, sc in same place as sl st, * ch 5, sk next dc, sc in next dc. Rep from * around; join to first sc. Fasten off.

Rnd 3: Join A to any lp, sc in same lp, * **ch 4; holding back on hook the last lp of each trc make 3 trc in same lp, thread over and draw through all lps on hook— cluster (cl) made; ch 5, sl st in tip of cl—picot made;** ch 4, sc in same lp, ch 5, sc in next lp. Rep from * around; join with sl st to first sc. Fasten off.

Rnd 4: Join MC to any picot, sc in same sp, * ch 10, dc in next lp, ch 10, sc in next picot. Rep from * around; join.

Rnd 5: Sl st to center of next lp, sc in same sp, ch 11, sc in next lp, ch 5, sc in second sp preceding trc-grp on center, ch 5, sc in next lp on flower motif, ch 5, sk 2 sps on center, sc in next sp, ch 5, sc in next lp on flower motif, ch 5, sc in next sp on center, ch 5, sc in next lp on flower motif, ch 5, sk 2 sps on center, sc in next sp, ch 5, sc in next lp on flower motif, * ch 11, sc in next lp. Rep from * around; join. Fasten off.

Make 4 more flower motifs, joining to center as before.

Fill-in motif: With B, work Rnd 1 as for flower motif.

Rnd 2: Sc in same place as sl st, * ch 2, sl st in center trc of any trc-grp on center, ch 2, sk next dc on motif, sc in next dc, * ch 5, sk next dc, sc in next dc. Rep from * around; join. Fasten off. Make a fill-in motif over each trc-grp.

Edging: Work in rnds as follows: *Rnd 1:* Join MC to third free lp following joining on fill-in motif, sc in same place, * (ch 7, sc in next lp) 5 times; ch 3, trc in next lp, trc in next sp on center, sc in first free lp on flower motif, ch 5, sl st in last ch-7 lp made on fill-in motif, ch 5, sc in next lp on flower motif, (ch 11, sc in next lp) 14 times; trc in next sp on center, trc in first lp on next fill-in motif, ch 3, sc in next lp, ch 3, sl st in last ch-11 lp on previous flower motif, ch 3, sc in next lp on fill-in motif. Rep from * around; join.

Rnd 2: Sl st to center of next lp on fill-in motif, ch 4, 3-trc cl in same lp, * (ch 6, 4-trc cl in next lp) 3 times; 4-trc cl in next free lp on flower motif, (ch 6, 4-trc cl in next lp) 12 times; 4-trc cl in next free lp on fill-in motif. Rep from * around; join to tip of first cl.

Rnd 3: Sl st in next sp, ch 3, 5 dc in same sp, 6 dc in each of next 3 sps, * 8 dc in each of next 12 sps, 6 dc in each of next 5 sps. Rep from * around; join to top of ch-3.

Rnd 4: Sc in same place as sl st, * ch 5, sk next dc, sc in next dc. Rep from * around; join.

Rnd 5: Sl st to center of next lp, sc in same place, * ch 5, sc in next lp. Rep from * around; join.

Rnds 6-7: Work same as Rnd 5, making ch-6 lps on Rnd 6 and ch-7 lps on Rnd 7. Fasten off at end of Rnd 7.

Rnd 8: Join B to any lp, work as before, making ch-8 lps around; join. Fasten off.

Rnd 9: Join A to any lp, work as before, making ch-9 lps around; join. Fasten off. Starch lightly and press, ruffling edging.

Large Pineapple Doily
Shown on page 6

The diameter of the finished doily in the thread recommended below is 28 inches. For a smaller (24-inch-diameter) centerpiece, substitute three 300-yard balls of

Clark's Big Ball white crochet cotton, Size 20, and a Size 9 steel crochet hook.

MATERIALS

- J. & P. Coats Knit-Cro-Sheen mercerized crochet cotton: 4 (250-yard) balls of white
- Size 7 steel crochet hook

Abbreviations: See pages 26-27.

INSTRUCTIONS

Ch 9, sl st to form ring.

Rnd 1: Ch 4, (dc in ring, ch 1) 15 times; join with sl st in third st of ch-4.

Rnd 2: Ch 5, (dc in next dc, ch 2) around; join in third st of ch-5.

Rnd 3: Ch 3, 2 dc in sp, (dc in next dc, 2 dc in next sp) around; join in top of ch-3.

Rnd 4: Ch 3, dc in same place, (ch 3, sk next 2 sts, 2 dc in next st) around; ch 3, join in top of ch-3—16 ch-3 sps made.

Rnd 5: Ch 3, dc in next dc, (ch 4, dc in each of next 2 dc) around; ch 4; join.

Rnd 6: Ch 3, dc in next dc, (5 dc in next sp, dc in each of next 2 dc) around, 5 dc in last sp; join.

Rnd 7: Ch 3, 2 dc in next dc, (ch 5, sk 5 st, dc in next dc, 2 dc in next dc) around; end ch 5; join.

Rnd 8: Ch 3, dc in each of next 2 dc, (ch 6, dc in each of next 3 dc) around; end ch 6; join.

Rnd 9: Work same as Rnd 8, having ch-7 instead of ch-6.

Rnd 10: Ch 3, dc in each of next 2 dc, (8 dc in sp, dc in each of next 3 dc) around; 8 dc in last sp; join.

Rnd 11: Ch 3, 2 dc in next dc, dc in next dc; (ch 7, sk next 8 sts, dc in dc, 2 dc in next dc, dc in next dc) around; end ch 7; join.

Rnd 12: Ch 3, dc in each of next 3 dc, (ch 8, dc in each of next 4 dc) around; end ch 8; join.

Rnd 13: Work same as Rnd 12, having ch-9 instead of ch-8.

Rnd 14: Ch 3, dc in each of next 3 dc, (9 dc in ch-9 lp, dc in each of next 4 dc) around; 9 dc in last sp; join.

Rnd 15: Ch 3, dc in each of next 3 dc, (ch 5, sk next 4 dc, dc in next st, ch 5, sk 4 sts, dc in each of next 4 sts) around; end ch 5; join.

Rnd 16: Ch 3, dc in each of next 3 dc, (ch 5, **in next dc make dc, ch 2, dc—V st made;** ch 5, dc in each of next 4 dc) around; end ch 5; join.

Rnd 17: Work same as Rnd 16, making dc, ch 2, dc in ch-2 lp.

Rnds 18-19: Ch 3, dc in each of next 4 dc, (ch 6, in ch-2 lp make dc, ch 2, dc; ch 6, dc in each of next 4 dc) around; end ch 6; join.

Rnds 20-21: Work same as Rnd 18, having ch-7 instead of ch-6.

Rnds 22-23: Ch 3, dc in next dc, (ch 2, dc in each of next 2 dc, ch 7, in ch-2 lp make V st; ch 7, dc in next 2 dc of the 4-dc grp) around; end ch 7; join to top of ch 3.

Rnd 24: Ch 5, dc in next st, (dc in next dc, ch 2, dc in next dc, ch 7, in ch-2 lp make V st; ch 7, skip dc, dc in next dc, ch 2, dc in next dc) around; end ch 7; join with sl st to third ch of ch-5.

Rnds 25-26: Sl st into ch-2 lp, **ch 3, dc in same sp, ch 2, 2 dc in same sp—beg shell made;** in next ch-2 sp make **2 dc, ch 2, 2 dc— shell made;** (ch 6, in ch-2 sp make V st; ch 6, shell in each of next 2 ch-2 sps) around; join.

Rnds 27-29: Work same as Rnd 26, having ch-7 instead of ch-6.

Rnd 30: [(Shell in shell) twice; ch 6, in ch-2 sp make dc, ch 7, dc; ch 6] around; join.

Rnd 31: [(Shell in shell) twice; ch 5, 11 dc in ch-7 lp, ch 5] around; join.

Rnd 32: [(Shell in shell) twice; ch 4, making ch-1 bet each dc, dc in each of 11 dc, ch 4] around; join.

Rnd 33: [(Shell in shell) twice; ch 5, sc in first ch-1 sp, (ch 3, sc in next sp) 9 times, ch 5—9 lps on pineapple] around; end ch 5; join.

Note: Hereafter, repeat the directions given for each rnd.

Rnds 34-35: Shell in shell, ch 1, shell in shell, ch 5, sc in ch-3 lp, (ch 3, sc in next lp) across pineapple, ch 5. *Rnd 36:* Shell in shell, dc in ch-1 sp, shell in shell, ch 5, make 6 lps across pineapple, ch 5.

Rnd 37: Shell in shell, in dc work V st; shell in shell, ch 5, make 5 lps across pineapple, ch 5.

Rnd 38: Shell in shell, ch 2, in ch-2 sp make V st; ch 2, shell in shell, ch 5, make 4 lps across pineapple, ch 5.

Rnd 39: Shell in shell, ch 3, in ch-2 sp of V st make dc, ch 11, dc; ch 3, shell in shell, ch 5, make 3 lps across pineapple, ch 5.

Rnd 40: Shell in shell, ch 4, 14 dc in ch-11 lp, ch 4, shell in shell, ch 5, make 2 lps across pineapple, ch 5.

Rnd 41: Shell in shell, ch 5; making ch 1 bet each dc, dc in each dc of 14-dc grp; ch 5, shell in shell, ch 5, make 1 lp across pineapple, ch 5.

Rnd 42: Shell in shell, ch 5, make 12 ch-3 lps across pineapple, ch 5, shell in shell, ch 5, sc in ch-3 lp, ch 5. *Rnds 43-45:* Shell in shell, ch 5, make ch-3 lps across pineapple, ch 5, shell in shell, ch 2.

Rnd 46: Shell in shell, ch 5, make 8 lps across pineapple, ch 5, shell in shell, ch 7.

Rnd 47: Shell in shell, ch 5, 7 lps across pineapple, ch 5, shell in shell, 10 dc over ch-7.

Rnds 48-49: Shell in shell, ch 5, make ch-3 lps across pineapple, ch 5, shell in shell, dc in first dc, (ch 1, dc in next dc) 9 times.

Rnd 50: Shell in shell, ch 5, make 4 lps across pineapple. ch 5, shell in shell, (ch 2, trc in next dc) 10 times, ch 2. *Rnd 51:* Shell in shell, ch 5, make 3 lps across pineapple, ch 5, shell in shell, (ch 3, trc in next trc) 10 times, ch 3.

Rnds 52-53: Shell in shell, ch 5, make ch-3 lps across pineapple, ch 5, shell in shell (ch 4, trc in next trc) 10 times, ch 4. *Rnd 54:* Shell in shell, ch 3, sc in ch-3 sp, ch 3, 2 dc in next shell, ch 1, sl st back into ch-2 sp of previous shell made, ch 1, complete shell, (ch 5, trc in next trc, ch 3, sl st in top of trc just made) 10 times, ch 5. Continue around, join in top of first shell made. Fasten off.

Centerpiece Doily With Violets
Shown on page 7

Finished doily measures 24 inches in diameter.

MATERIALS
- J. & P. Coats Knit-Cro-Sheen (or a suitable substitute): 2 large (400-yard) balls
- Size 9 steel crochet hook

Abbreviations: See pages 26-27.

INSTRUCTIONS
Ch 8, join with sl st to form ring.

Rnd 1: Ch 3 (to count as first dc), 23 dc in ring. Join with sl st to top of ch-3.

Rnd 2: Ch 5, sk 1 dc, dc in next dc, * ch 2, sk 1 dc, dc in next dc. Rep. from * around. Join last ch 2 with sl st in third ch of first ch-5—12 sps made.

Rnd 3: Sl st in sp, ch 3, 2 dc in same sp, * ch 2, 3 dc in next sp. Rep from * around joining last ch 2 to top of first ch-3—twelve 3-dc groups made.

Rnd 4: Ch 3, 2 dc in next dc, dc in next dc, * ch 1, 2 dc in next sp, ch 1, 2 dc in next dc, dc in next 2 dc. Rep from * around, joining last ch 1 to top of ch-2—24 sp made.

Rnd 5: Ch 3, dc in each of next 3 dc, * ch 1, dc in next 2 dc, ch 1, dc in next 4 dc. Rep from * around. Join as on last rnd.

Rnd 6: Rep Rnd 5.

Rnd 7: Ch 3, dc in 3 dc, * (ch 1, dc in next dc) twice; ch 1, dc in 4 dc. Rep from * around. Join.

Rnd 8: Ch 3, dc in each of next 3 dc, * ch 1, sk 1 dc, in next ch-1 sp make **dc, ch 2 and dc—V st made;** ch 1, sk 1 dc, dc in each of next 4 dc. Rep from * around. Join.

Rnd 9: Ch 3, dc in 3 dc, * ch 2, sk 1 dc, 3 dc in ch-2 sp of V-st, ch 2, sk 1 dc, dc in each of next 4 dc. Rep from * around. Join.

Rnd 10: Ch 3, dc in 2 dc, 2 dc in next dc, * ch 2, dc in 2 dc, 2 dc in next dc, ch 2, dc in each of next 3 dc, 2 dc in next dc. Rep from * around. Join.

Rnd 11: Ch 3, dc in each of next 3 dc, 2 dc in next dc, * ch 3, sk 1 dc, **holding back on hook the last lp of each dc, make dc in next 3 dc, yo and draw through all 4 lps on hook—3-dc cluster made;** ch 3, dc in each of next 4 dc, 2 dc in next dc. Rep from * around. Join.

Rnd 12: Ch 3, dc in each of next 4 dc, 2 dc in next dc, * (ch 3, dc in next sp) twice; ch 3, dc in each of next 5 dc, 2 dc in next dc. Rep from * around. Join.

Rnd 13: Ch 3, sk next dc, dc in each of next 5 dc, * (ch 3, dc in next sp) 3 times; ch 3, sk next dc, dc in each of next 6 dc. Rep from * around. Join.

Rnd 14: Ch 3, sk next dc, dc in each of next 4 dc, * (ch 3, dc in sp) 4 times; ch 3, skip next dc, dc in each of next 5 dc. Rep from * around. Join.

Rnd 15: Ch 3, sk next dc, dc in each of next 3 dc, * (ch 3, dc in next sp) 5 times; ch 3, sk next dc, dc in each of next 4 dc. Rep from * around. Join.

Rnd 16: Ch 3, sk 1 dc, **holding back last loop on hook, dc in next 2 dc, yo and draw through 3 lps on hook—2-dc cluster made,** * (ch 3, dc in next sp) 6 times; ch 3, sk 1 dc, make a 3-dc cluster over next 3 dc. Rep from * around. Join to top of first cluster.

Rnd 17: Sl st in next ch and into same sp, ch 6, dc in next sp, * ch 3, dc in next sp. Rep from * around. Join to third ch of starting ch-6—84 sps around.

Rnd 18: Rep Rnd 17.

Rnd 19: Ch 3, * (3 dc in sp, dc in dc) twice; (ch 3, dc in next dc) twice. Rep from * around. Join.

Rnd 20: Ch 3, * dc in each of next 3 dc, V st in next dc, dc in each of next 4 dc, (ch 2, dc in next dc) twice. Rep from * around. Join.

Rnd 21: Ch 3, dc in each of next 4 dc, * work V st in ch-2 sp of V st, dc in each of next 5 dc, ch 2, V st in next dc, ch 2, dc in 5 dc. Rep from * around. Join.

Rnd 22: Ch 3, dc in 4 dc, * ch 2, sk 2 dc of V st, dc in each of next 5 dc, ch 1, 3 dc in ch-2 sp of V st, ch 1, dc in each of next 5 dc. Rep from * around. Join.

Rnd 23: Sl st in next dc, ch 3, dc in each of next 3 dc, * ch 2, dc in each of next 4 dc, ch 1, sk 1 dc, dc in each of next 3 dc, ch 1, sk next dc, dc in each of next 4 dc. Rep from * around. Join.

Rnd 24: Sl st in next dc, ch 3, dc in each of next 2 dc, * ch 3, dc in each of next 3 dc, ch 1, sk 1 dc, dc in each of next 2 dc, 2 dc in next dc, ch 1, sk 1 dc, dc in each of next 3 dc. Rep from * around. Join.

Rnd 25: Sl st in next dc, ch 3, dc in next dc, * ch 3, dc in each of next 2 dc, ch 2, sk 1 dc, dc in next 3 dc, 2 dc in next dc, ch 2, sk 1 dc, dc in each of next 2 dc. Rep from * around, ending with ch 2; join to top of ch-3.

Rnd 26: Sl st in next dc, ch 6, sk 1 dc, dc in next dc, * ch 3, dc in each of next 4 dc, 2 dc in next dc, (ch 3, sk 1 dc, dc in next dc) twice. Rep from * around, ending with ch 3; join to third ch of ch-6.

Rnd 27: Sl st in 2 ch, ch 5, dc in next sp, * ch 2, dc in each of next 5 dc, 2 dc in next dc, ch 2, (dc in next sp, ch 3) twice; dc in next sp. Rep from * around, ending with ch 3. Join to third ch of ch-5.

Rnd 28: Sl st in 2 ch, ch 6, sk 1 dc, * dc in each of next 6 dc, 2 dc in next dc, ch 3, sk 1 dc, dc in next sp, ch 3, dc in next sp, ch 3, sk 1 dc. Rep from * around. Join.

Rnd 29: Sl st in 2 ch, ch 6, sk 1 dc, * dc in each of next 7 dc, (ch 3, dc in next sp) 3 times; ch 3, sk 1 dc. Rep from * around. Join—4 ch-3 lps between dc grps.

Rnd 30: Sl st in 2 ch, ch 6, sk 1 dc, * dc in each rem dc of this group, (ch 3, dc in next sp) to within next group, ch 3, sk 1 dc. Rep from * around. Join—5 ch-3 lps between dc grps.

Rnd 31-33: Rep Rnd 30.

Rnd 34: Sl st in 2 ch, ch 6, sk 1 dc, * make a 2-dc cluster over next 2 dc, (ch 3, dc in next sp) 8 times, ch 3, sk 1 dc. Rep from * around. Join—189 ch-3 lps around.

Rnd 35: Sl st in 2 ch, ch 3, 2 dc in same sp, ch 2, dc in top of next cl, * ch 2, 3 dc in next sp, ch 2, dc in next sp, rep from * around. Join.

Rnd 36: Sl st in next dc, ch 3, dc in next dc, * ch 3, dc in next dc, ch 3, sk 1 dc, 2-dc cluster over next 2 dc. Rep from * around. Join.

Rnd 37: Ch 1, sc in same place as joining sl st, * ch 5, sc in next dc, ch 5, sc in top of cluster. Rep from * around. Join to first sc.

Rnd 38: Sl st in 2 ch, ch 1, sc in same lp, * ch 2, V st in next lp, ch 2, sc in next lp. Rep from * around. Join.

Rnd 39: Sl st in next ch, ch 5, * V st in sp of next V st, ch 2, dc in each of next 2 sps, ch 2. Rep from * around. Join last dc to third ch of starting ch-5.

Rnd 40: Ch 1, sc in same place as joining sl st, * ch 2, in sp of next V st make **2 dc, ch 2 and 2 dc—2-dc shell made;** ch 2, sk 2 dc, sc in next dc. Rep from * around. Join.

Rnd 41: Sl st in next ch, ch 5, * make 3 dc, ch 2, 3 dc in sp of next shell, ch 2, dc in each of next 2 sps, ch 2. Rep from * around. Join with sl st to third ch of ch-5.

Rnd 42: Ch 1, sc in next sp, * ch 2, 3 dc, ch 2, 3 dc in sp of next shell, ch 2, sc in each of next 2 sps. Rep from * around. Join and fasten off.

Five-Sided Pineapple Doily
Shown on page 7

Finished size of doily is 21 inches in diameter.

——————**MATERIALS**——————
• Coats & Clark Red Heart Lustersheen: 2 (2-ounce) skeins white
• Size E aluminum crochet hook

Abbreviations: See pages 26-27.

——————**INSTRUCTIONS**——————
Ch 10; join with sl st to form ring.
Rnd 1: Ch 3, dc in ring, (ch 2, 2 dc in ring) 9 times; ch 2, join with sl st to top of beg ch-3.

Rnd 2: **Sl st in dc and in ch-2 sp, ch 3, dc in same sp, ch 2, 2 dc in same sp—beg shell made;** (in next ch-2 sp make **shell of 2 dc, ch 2, and 2 dc**) 9 times; join to top of ch-3.

Rnd 3: Make beg shell in center of shell, (ch 1, shell in next shell) 9 times; ch 1, join in top of ch-3.

Note: All rnds in pat start with beg shell.

Rnd 4: * Shell in shell, ch 2, make (2 dc, ch 2, 2 dc, ch 2, and 2 dc) in next shell, ch 2. Rep from * around; join. *Rnd 5:* (Shell in shell, ch 3, sk ch-2 sp, shell in each of next 2 ch-2 sps, ch 3) around; join. *Rnd 6:* (Shell in shell, ch 3) around; join.

Rnd 7: * (Shell in shell, ch 3) twice, dc in ch-3 sp, ch 3, shell in shell, ch 3. Rep from * around; join.

Rnd 8: * (Shell in shell, ch 3) twice; make (dc, ch 5, dc) in center dc, ch 3, shell in shell, ch 3. Rep from * around; join.

Rnd 9: * (Shell in shell, ch 3) twice; 10 dc in ch-5 sp, ch 3, shell in shell, ch 3. Rep from * around; join.

Rnd 10: Make beg shell, ch 2, 2 dc in same sp, * ch 3, shell in next shell, ch 3, dc in first dc of 10 dc-group, (ch 1, dc in next dc) 9 times; ch 3, shell in shell, ch 3, make (2 dc, ch 2, 2 dc, ch 2, 2 dc) in next shell. Rep from * around; join.

Rnd 11: * (Shell in shell) twice, ch 3, shell in shell, ch 3, sc in ch-1 sp, (ch 3, sc in next sp) 8 times; ch 3, shell in shell, ch 3. Rep from * around; join.

Rnd 12: * (Shell in shell, ch 3) 3 times; sc in ch-3 lp, (ch 3, sc in next lp) 7 times; ch 3, shell in shell, ch 3. Rep from * around; join.

Rnd 13: * Shell in shell, ch 1, 5 dc in ch-3 sp, ch 1, (shell in shell, ch 3) twice; work 6 lps across pineapple, ch 3, shell in shell, ch 3. Rep from * around; join.

Rnd 14: * Shell in shell, ch 1, sk 2 dc, 2 dc in each of next 5 dc, ch 1, (shell in shell, ch 3) twice; work 5 lps across pineapple, ch 3, shell in shell, ch 3. Rep from * around; join.

Rnd 15: * Shell in shell, ch 1, sk 2 dc (dc in next dc, ch 1) 10 times; (shell in shell, ch 3) twice; work 4 lps across pineapple, ch 3, shell in shell, ch 3. Rep from * around; join.

Rnd 16: * Shell in shell, ch 2, sk 2 dc, (dc in next dc, ch 2) 10 times; (shell in shell, ch 3) twice; make 3 lps across pineapple, ch 3, shell in shell, ch 3. Rep from * around; join.

Rnd 17: * Shell in shell, (ch 3, dc in next dc) 10 times, (ch 3, shell in shell) twice; ch 3, make 2 lps across pineapple, ch 3, shell in shell, ch 3. Rep from * around; join.

Rnd 18: * Shell in shell, (shell in next ch-3 lp) 11 times; (shell in shell, ch 3) twice; make 1 lp in pineapple, ch 3, shell in shell, ch 3. Rep from * around; join.

Rnd 19: * (Shell in shell) 13 times; ch 3, shell in shell, ch 3, sc in center lp, ch 3, shell in shell, ch 3. Rep from * around; join.

Rnd 20: * (Shell in shell) 13 times; ch 3, (shell in shell) twice; ch 3. Rep from * around; join.

Rnd 21: * (Shell in shell) 13 times; (ch 3, 2 dc in center of next shell) twice; ch 3. Rep from * around; join.

Rnd 22: Sl st to center of shell, ch 3 and make dc in same sp, **ch 3, sl st in top of dc just made for picot,** 2 dc in same sp, * (ch 2, in next shell make 2 dc, picot, 2 dc) 12 times; ch 2, make (2 dc, picot, 2 dc) in each of next 3 ch-3 sps, ch 2, make (2 dc, picot, 2 dc) in next shell. Rep from * around; join last ch-2 to top of beg ch-3. Fasten off.

To block, use wool setting on steam iron. Press wrong side of work carefully, beginning at center of doily and working outward.

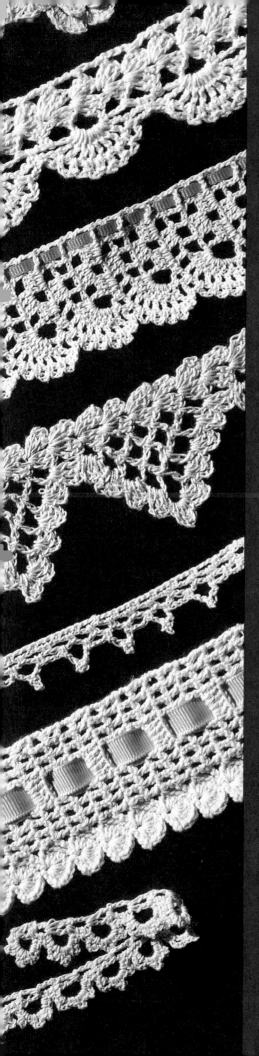

BEST-LOVED EDGINGS

for a personal touch

Beautiful crocheted edgings are
the perfect finish for many fashion and home
furnishings accessories. Whether you
prefer lacy trims worked in traditional
crochet cottons or more robust
edgings crocheted in heavier threads and
yarns, here and on the next two pages you're
sure to find several designs to suit
your stitching skills and turn
even a token gift into a treasure.

The delicate edgings shown here
are ½ to 3¾ inches wide. From the top,
they include the Irish rose, a
scalloped design, filet trim with scallops
a triangular edging, a slender
picot-edged pattern (this same design
is worked in heavier thread at far left),
a beribboned mesh edging with
scallops, and a narrow crown motif trim.
Instructions begin on page 20.

◆ ◆ ◆

Lustrous cotton threads will work up beautifully into the glamorous edgings used on the scarf, *left,* and napkins, *below.* The quick-to-make scarf edging features only two rows of crochet worked in an airy shell pattern.

The napkins (sewn from men's handkerchiefs) are trimmed with edgings ranging from 1 to 2 inches wide. These are a mesh and picot trim, *top left,* slanted scallop edging, *bottom left,* picot-trimmed triangle, *bottom right,* and cloverleaf edging, *in the basket.*

Leftover yarns are all that's needed to create the spectacular skirt border, *opposite.* Traditionally worked in delicate threads, this deeply scalloped border takes on an entirely new look when it is worked in yarn. Directions for fitting the edging to a finished garment also are included in these instructions.

Irish Rose Edging
Shown on page 16

Finished size is approximately 3¾ inches wide.

MATERIALS
- J. & P. Coats Knit-Cro-Sheen: 1 (250-yard) ball of ecru
- Size 7 steel crochet hook

Abbreviations: See pages 26-27.

INSTRUCTIONS
Ch 7, join with sl st to form ring.

Rnd 1: Ch 6, dc in ring, (ch 3, dc in ring) 6 times; ch 3, join to third ch of ch-6 at beg of rnd—8 ch-3 lps.

Rnd 2: Ch 1, in each ch-3 lp around work (sc, 3 dc, sc); do not join.

Rnd 3: (Sl st from the back, around the post of next dc of previous row, ch 6) 8 times; do not join.

Rnd 4: In each ch-6 lp around work sc, hdc, 5 dc, hdc, sc; join with sl st to first sc. Fasten off.

Work a second rose through Rnd 3, then join to first rose as follows:

In ch-6 lp work sc, hdc, 2 dc, sl st to center st of any petal of first rose, make 3 dc, hdc, and sc in same lp on rose in progress; make sc, hdc, 2 dc, in next lp, join to center st of next petal on first rose; make 3 dc, hdc, sc in same lp and finish rose same as first rose.

Continue to make roses and join in same manner, leaving two free petals on each side for desired length.

Heading: Join thread along edge in center st of second free petal to the right of rose joining, * ch 7, sc in center st of next petal, ch 7, sc in same st used to join 2 petals; ch 7, sc in center st of first petal in next rose and rep from * across row; ch 9, turn.

Row 2: Sc in first loop, * ch 7, sc in next lp, rep from * across row; ch 9, turn.

Rows 3-6: Rep Row 2; ending Row 6 with ch 1, turn.

Row 7: In each ch-7 lp work 7 sc. Fasten off.

Scalloped Design
Shown on page 16

Finished size is approximately 1½ inches wide.

MATERIALS
- DMC Cordonnet, Size 10: 1 (124-yard) ball of ecru
- Size 7 steel crochet hook

Abbreviations: See pages 26-27.

INSTRUCTIONS
Ch 5. *Row 1:* In fifth ch from hook make **3 dc, ch 2, 3 dc—shell made;** ch 4, turn.

Row 2: In ch-2 lp of shell make **3 dc, ch 2, 3 dc—shell in shell made;** skip 2 dc, trc in next dc; ch 4, turn.

Row 3: Make shell in shell, trc in turning ch-4 lp 2 rows below; ch 4, turn.

Repeat *Row 3* for desired length.

Scallop edging: Sl st into lp just made, ch 5, (in same lp make trc, ch 1) 8 times; * ch 1, skip lp, sc in next lp, ch 2, skip lp, (in next lp make trc, ch 1) 9 times, rep from * across row; ch 2, turn.

Next row: Sc between next 2 trc, * (ch 3, sc between next 2 trc) 7 times; ch 3, sl st in next sc, ch 3, sc between next 2 trc, rep from * across row. Fasten off.

Filet Trim with Scallops
Shown on page 16

Finished size is approximately 1¾ inches wide.

MATERIALS
- DMC Cordonnet, Size 10: 1 (124-yard) ball of ecru
- Size 7 steel crochet hook

Abbreviations: See pages 26-27.

INSTRUCTIONS
Ch 21. *Row 1:* Dc in eighth ch from hook, ch 2, sk 2 ch, dc in each of next 4 ch; ch 2, sk 2 ch, dc in next ch, ch 4, sl st in last ch; ch 2, turn.

Row 2: Work 7 dc in ch-4 lp, ch 2, sk dc and ch-2 sp, dc in next dc, ch 2, sk 2 dc, dc in next dc; ch 2, dc in next dc, ch 2, sk 2 ch, dc in next ch; ch 5, turn.

Row 3: Dc in next dc, ch 2, dc in next dc, 2 dc in ch-2 sp, dc in next dc; ch 2, dc in next sp, ch 1, sk next dc, (dc in next dc, ch 1) 6 times; dc in top of ch-2; ch 3, turn.

Row 4: Sc in first ch-1 lp, ch 3, (sc in next lp, ch 3) 5 times; sc in next lp, sl st in top of next dc; ch 2, 2 dc in ch-2 lp, dc in next dc; ch 2, sk 2 dc, dc in next dc; 2 dc in ch-2 lp, dc in next dc; ch 2, sk 2 ch, dc in next ch; ch 5, turn.

Row 5: Dc in next dc, ch 2, sk 2 dc, dc in next dc; 2 dc in ch-2 lp, dc in next dc; ch 2, skip 2 dc, dc in top of ch-2; ch 4, sc in first ch-3 lp of scallop to left; ch 2, turn.

Row 6: Rep Row 2.

Row 7: Dc in next dc, ch 2, dc in next dc, 2 dc in ch-2 sp, dc in next dc; ch 2, dc in next sp; ch 1, sk dc (dc in next dc, ch 1) 6 times; dc in top of ch-2; sc in third ch-3 lp of scallop to left; ch 3, turn.

Row 8: Rep Row 4.

Rep Rows 5-8 until desired length is reached, breaking off thread after sl st in Rnd 4.

Press and block edging.

Triangular Edging
Shown on page 16

Finished size is approximately 2 inches wide.

MATERIALS
- Clark's Big Ball, Size 20: 1 ball of ecru
- Size 9 steel crochet hook

Abbreviations: See pages 26-27.

INSTRUCTIONS
Starting at narrow edge, ch 4.

Row 1: In fourth ch from hook make 2 dc, ch 1, 3 dc; ch 5, turn.

Row 2: Sk first 3 dc, in next ch-1 sp make 3 dc, ch 1, 3 dc; ch 1, turn.

Row 3: Sk first dc, sl st in each of next 2 dc, sl st in next ch-1 st; ch 3, in same sp make 2 dc, ch 1, 3 dc; ch 2, sk next 2 dc, dc in next dc, ch 2, dc in third ch of turning-ch; ch 5, turn.

Row 4: Sk first dc, (dc in next dc, ch 2) twice; sk next 2 dc, in next ch-1 sp make 3 dc, ch 1, 3 dc; ch 1, turn.

Row 5: Sk first dc, sl st in each of next 2 dc, sl st in next ch-1 sp; ch 3, in same sp make 2 dc, ch 1, 3 dc; ch 2, sk next 2 dc, dc in next dc; (ch 2, dc in next dc) twice; ch 2, dc in third ch of turning-ch; ch 5, turn.

Row 6: Sk first dc, (dc in next dc, ch 2) 4 times; sk next 2 dc, in next ch-1 sp make 3 dc, ch 1, 3 dc; ch 1, turn.

Row 7: Sk first dc, sl st in each of next 2 dc, sl st in next ch-1 sp; ch 3, in same sp make 2 dc, ch 1, 3 dc; ch 5, turn.

Rep Rows 2-7 for pattern. Work in pattern for desired length, ending with sixth row. Break off.

Heading: With right side facing and working along pointed edge, attach thread to first ch-2 sp, in same sp make sc, ch 3, 2 dc; (in next sp make sc, ch 3, 2 dc) 3 times; * in next sp at tip of triangle make (sc, ch 3, 2 dc) twice; (in next sp make sc, ch 3, 2 dc) 8 times. Rep from * across, ending in pattern as established. Fasten off.

Press and block edging.

Picot-Edged Pattern
Shown on pages 16 and 17

This edging is worked in two different threads. Finished width of the edging worked in the heavier thread, *page 16,* is ¾ inch; width of the edging in lighter thread, *page 17,* is ½ inch. The materials list below includes threads and hook sizes for both widths, with the narrower width in parentheses. Directions are the same for both widths.

——————— MATERIALS ———————
• DMC Cordonnet, Size 10 (Size 20): 1 (124-yard) ball of ecru
• Size 7 (Size 9) steel crochet hook

Abbreviations: See pages 26-27.

——————— INSTRUCTIONS ———————
Make a chain slightly longer than length desired for finished edging.

Row 1: Sc in sixth ch from hook, * ch 3, sk 2 ch, sc in next ch; rep from * across, ending with ch 1, dc in last ch, having number of loops divisible by 3, plus 2 more loops. Ch 3, turn.

Row 2: * Sc in next loop, ch 3; rep from * across, ending with ch 1, dc in last loop; ch 6, turn.

Row 3: **Sc in fourth ch from hook—picot made,** * ch 2, sc in next loop, ch 3, sc in next loop, ch 6, make picot; rep from * across. Break off.

Press and block edging.

Mesh Edging with Scallops
Shown on page 16

Finished size is approximately 2 inches wide.

——————— MATERIALS ———————
• J. & P. Coats Knit Cro-Sheen: 1 (250-yard) ball of ecru
• Size 8 steel crochet hook

Abbreviations: See pages 26-27.

——————— INSTRUCTIONS ———————
Ch 24. *Row 1:* Dc in fourth ch from hook, **make 9 dc in same ch —first shell made;** skip 2 ch, dc in next ch; (ch 1, sk ch, dc in next ch) 3 times; dc in next 5 ch; (ch 1, sk ch, dc in next ch) 3 times; ch 4, turn.

Row 2: Sk first dc, (dc in next dc, ch 1) twice; dc in next dc, ch 4, sk 4 dc; (dc in next dc, ch 1) 3 times; dc in next dc, ch 3, sc in sixth dc of shell group; ch 3, turn.

Row 3: Make 10 dc in sc just made; (dc in next dc, ch 1) 3 times, dc in next dc; 4 dc in ch-4 lp, (dc in next dc, ch 1) 3 times; dc in third ch of turning ch-4 lp; ch 4, turn.

Rep Rows 2-3 for desired length. Fasten off.

Press and block edging.

Crown Motif Trim
Shown on page 17

Finished size is approximately ½ inch wide.

——————— MATERIALS ———————
• DMC Cordonnet, Size 20: 1 (174-yard) ball of ecru
• Size 9 steel crochet hook

Abbreviations: See pages 26-27.

——————— INSTRUCTIONS ———————
Starting at narrow end, ch 7. *Row 1:* In seventh ch from hook make dc, ch 1, and dc; ch 4, turn.

Row 2: Dc in ch-1 sp; ch 7, turn.

Row 3: In turning ch-4 sp make dc, ch 1 and dc; ch 4, turn.

Rep Rows 2 and 3 until piece is slightly longer than desired length; end with Row 3. Ch 1, turn.

Now work across long side as follows: * In next ch-7 loop make (2 sc, ch 3) 3 times, 2 sc in same lp; sc in side of next dc. Rep from * across. Break off.

Press and block edging.

Scarf Edging
Shown on page 18

Finished size is approximately 1 inch wide.

——————— MATERIALS ———————
• Scarf or large handkerchief
• DMC Brilliant Crochet Cotton: 1 (218-yard) ball of white
• Size 6 steel crochet hook
• White sewing thread

Abbreviations: See pages 26-27.

——————— INSTRUCTIONS ———————
Measure along the outside edge of the scarf or handkerchief. Total the length of the four sides to determine the length of the edging, then add a little extra length to the edging to allow for ease when turning the corners.

Edging: *Row 1:* Ch desired length, sc in second ch from hook; (ch 5, sk 3 ch, sc in next ch). Rep across foundation ch. Fasten off.

continued

Row 2: With lp on hook, work the following all in first ch-5 lp at beg of Row 1: (**Dc, ch 2, dc, ch 5, sc in fourth ch from hook—picot made, ch 1, dc, ch 2, dc**) for shell; * sk next lp, shell in next ch-5 lp. Rep from * across. Fasten off.

Press with warm iron and hand-stitch to scarf with matching sewing thread.

Mesh and Picot Trim
Shown on page 18

Finished size is approximately 1¼ inches wide.

——MATERIALS——
· DMC pearl cotton, Size 5: 6 skeins in the color of your choice
· Size 6 steel crochet hook
· Man's plaid handkerchiefs

Abbreviations: See pages 26-27.

——INSTRUCTIONS——
Edging *(mesh strip):* Ch 15, * dc in ninth ch from hook, (ch 2, sk 2 ch, dc in next dc) twice—3 mesh made; ** ch 5, turn, dc in second dc, ch 2, dc in next dc, ch 2, sk 2 ch, dc in next ch. Rep from ** once—mesh block made; ch 24.

Rep from * for desired length, ending with completion of mesh block. Fasten off.

Row 1: Working along the top edge of mesh strip, (the edge with *no* ch-9 lps between the mesh blocks), sc in the sp of the first corner mesh of first block, * ch 11, sk next mesh, sc in sp of next corner mesh, ch 3, work a 2-trc petal bet next 2 blocks as follows: **yo hook twice, draw up a loop in center ch of ch-9 lp, (yo, draw through 2 loops on hook)** twice; **yo hook twice, draw up a loop in same ch, (yo, draw through 2 lps on hook) twice; yo, draw through 3 loops on hook—petal made;** ch 3, work a second petal in same ch, ch 3, sc in sp of first mesh of next block; rep from * across. Fasten off; do not turn.

Row 2: Sc in first sc at beg of Row 1, * in ch-11 lp work (5 sc, **ch 4, sl st in fourth ch from hook—picot made;** 2 sc, picot, 2 sc, picot, 5 sc); 4 sc in next ch-3 lp; in sp bet next two petals work (2 sc, picot, 2 sc); 4 sc in next ch-3 lp. Rep from * across; end with sc in last sc. Fasten off.

Heading: *Row 1:* Working along opposite side of edging, join thread in sp of first mesh and make 3 sc in each mesh of first block, * 6 sc in next sp, sc in same st as petals, 6 sc in next sp, 3 sc in each sp of next square. Rep from * across. Fasten off; do not turn.

Row 2: Join thread in first sc of Row 1, ch 5, * sk 2 sc, dc in next sc, ch 2. Rep from * across.

Press with warm iron and hand-stitch to handkerchief with matching sewing thread.

Slanted Scallop Edging
Shown on page 18

Finished size is approximately 1½ inches wide.

——MATERIALS——
· DMC pearl cotton, Size 5: 8 skeins in the color of your choice
· Size 6 steel crochet hook
· Man's plaid handkerchiefs

Abbreviations: See pages 26-27.

——INSTRUCTIONS——
Edging: *Row 1:* Ch 13, in seventh ch from hook make **dc, ch 2, dc—shell made;** ch 3, dc in each of last 2 chs of foundation ch; ch 3, turn.

Row 2: Dc in second dc, ch 3, **shell in ch-2 sp of shell—shell in shell made;** ch 3, 5 dc in turning-lp; ch 4, turn.

Row 3: Sc in first dc, hdc in next dc; 2 dc in each of next 3 dc; ch 2, dc in next ch-3 lp, ch 2, shell in shell, ch 3, sk next sp, dc in next dc, dc in top of ch-3; ch 3, turn.

Row 4: Dc in second dc, ch 3, shell in shell, ch 3, sk next sp, 5 dc in next sp; ch 4, turn.

Rep Rows 3-4 for desired length; end with Row 3.

Press with warm iron and hand-stitch to handkerchief with matching sewing thread.

Picot-Trimmed Triangle Edging
Shown on page 18

Finished size is approximately 1 inch wide.

——MATERIALS——
· DMC pearl cotton, Size 5: 5 skeins in the color of your choice
· Size 6 steel crochet hook
· Man's plaid handkerchief

Abbreviations: See pages 26-27.

——INSTRUCTIONS——
Edging: *Row 1:* Ch desired length, dc in eighth ch from hook; (ch 2, sk 2 ch, dc in next dc) across row. Fasten off; do not turn.

Row 2: Sc in first sp at beg of Row 1, ch 3; * in next sp make sc, (**ch 4, sl st in fourth ch from hook—picot made**) 3 times; sl st in same ch used to make first picot—triple picot made;** sc in same sp. Ch 3, sk next sp, sc in next dc; in next sp work (hdc, dc, trc); dtrc in next dc; ch 6, sc in fourth ch from hook; (ch 4, sc in fourth ch from hook) twice; dc in first free ch before first picot, trc in next free ch; dtrc in same dc as previous dtrc; in next sp work (trc, dc, hdc); sc in next dc; ch 3, sk next sp. Rep from * across.

Press with warm iron and hand-stitch to handkerchief with matching sewing thread.

Cloverleaf Edging
Shown on page 18

Finished size is approximately 2 inches wide.

―――――――MATERIALS―――――――
- DMC pearl cotton, Size 8: 3 balls in the color of your choice
- Size 8 steel crochet hook
- Man's plaid handkerchief

Abbreviations: See pages 26-27.

―――――――INSTRUCTIONS―――――――
Edging: *Row 1:* Ch 12, dc in fourth ch from hook, dc in next ch, ch 5; in last ch work (dc, ch 3) 3 times, dc in same ch; ch 1, turn.

Row 2: In next ch-3 sp work **sc, hdc, 3 dc, hdc, and sc—shell made;** shell in each of next 2 ch-3 sps, ch 5, dc in ch-5 lp, dc in each dc and top of turning-ch; ch 3, turn.

Row 3: Dc in second dc and in each rem dc, dc in ch-5 lp, ch 5, sk first shell, in second dc of next shell work (dc, ch 3) 3 times, dc in same st; ch 1, turn.

Row 4: Shell in each of next 3 sps, ch 5, dc in ch-5 lp, dc in each dc and top of turning ch; ch 3, turn.

Rows 5-8: Rep Rows 3-4 (having 1 more dc in each row than previous row) until 8 rows are completed—10 dc in eighth row.

Row 9: Dc in next 2 dc, ch 5, sk 6 dc, in next dc work (dc, ch 3) 3 times, dc in same st; ch 1, turn.

Rep Rows 2-9 for pat. Fasten off.

Scalloped Border
Shown on page 19

To maintain the crispness of line that makes traditional edgings, intended for fine thread, so attractive, use a somewhat smaller hook than you would normally use for the yarn you select. This will tighten the work, giving it additional weight and body if it is to be used for a sleeve or skirt border.

In planning such borders for skirts, sleeves, and other items, consider the length of fabric that the border is applied to. This is es-pecially important when the edging is made of motifs that cannot be halved. Before working the entire edging, work one or two motifs, including the header, if there is one. Measure the length along the header to determine the width of the motif. Divide the header width into the length of the fabric piece (the hem of the skirt or sleeve) to determine the number of motifs you need. If the number of multiples doesn't fit exactly, it's easier to adjust the length of the fabric than the length of the crocheted work. To adjust patterns, slash pattern pieces to make them fuller or narrower and cut fabric accordingly.

―――――――MATERIALS―――――――
- Manos del Uruguay Strya (3.5-ounce skeins), or a suitable substitute: 2 skeins of dark gray, 1 skein each of gold, green, red, and light gray
- Size F aluminum crochet hook, or size to obtain gauge
- Purchased pattern and fabric for a simple skirt

Abbreviations: See pages 26-27.
Gauge: Single scallop without heading = 5½ inches wide and 5 inches deep. Heading adds 1 inch to depth of border.

―――――――INSTRUCTIONS―――――――
First scallop: Beg at center of scallop with dark gray, ch 15; join with sl st to first ch.

Row 1: Ch 1, work 25 sc in ring. Join with sl st to first sc.

Row 2: Ch 5, (sk next sc, dc in next sc, ch 2) 5 times; sk next sc, in next sc work (dc, ch 3, dc—tip of scallop); (ch 2, sk next sc, dc in next sc) 6 times; ch 1, turn.

Note: Pattern now works back and forth in rows.

Row 3: Sc in first dc, (2 sc in next ch-2 sp, sc in next dc) 6 times; 3 sc in ch-3 sp at tip of scallop, sc in next dc, (2 sc in next ch-2 sp, sc in next dc) 5 times, ending with 3 sc over turning ch; ch 1, turn.

Row 4: Sk first sc, sc in each sc to center sc at tip of scallop, 3 sc in center sc, sc in each sc to end; ch 1, turn.

Rows 5-7: Sk first st and work same as for Row 4.

Row 8: Without skipping st at beg of row, work same as for Row 4—47 sts; ch 1, turn.

Row 9: Sl st in first sc, ch 4, trc in same sc, (ch 3, sk 2 sc, **holding back the last lp of each trc, work 2 trc in next sc, yo, and draw through 3 lps on hook— trc cluster made**) 7 times; ch 3, in center sc work (trc cl, ch 3, trc cl); ch 3, sk sc, trc cl in next sc; (ch 3, sk 2 sc, trc cl in next sc) 7 times; ch 1, turn.

Row 10: In each ch-3 sp around work scallop of sc, 3 dc, and sc. Break off.

Second scallop: With gold, work same as for first scallop until Row 9 is completed; ch 1, turn.

Row 10: In each ch-3 sp around, work (sc, 3 dc, sc) to within last 2 ch-3 sps; (in next sp work sc, dc, drop lp from hook, insert hook on right side in corresponding dc on preceding scallop, draw dropped lp through, work 2 more dc and sc in same sp of scallop in progress) 2 times. Break off.

Continue making and joining scallops. Join last scallop to first scallop in first 2 ch-3 sps and to previous scallop in last 2 ch-3 sps.

Heading: *Rnd 1:* Working on the right side, across straight edge of scallops, attach yarn with sl st to last sc in Row 10 of first scallop; ch 5, * sk ½ inch on horizontal edge, dc in edge, ch 2. Rep from * across; ch 4, turn.

Rnd 2: Trc in first ch-2 sp, * ch 1, trc cl in next ch-2 sp. Rep from *, ending with trc cl in turning-ch; ch 1, turn.

Rnd 3: In each ch-1 sp make sc, dc, and sc, ending with sc in top of ch-4. Break off.

To finish: Cut out skirt pattern pieces and assemble skirt, following pattern instructions. Add edging to the finished hemline.

◆ ◆ ◆

Hooks, Yarns, and Stitchery Tips

◆ ◆ ◆

Here, and on the next few pages, you will find information and tips to increase your knowledge of crochet materials and equipment, improve your stitching technique and enhance your enjoyment of this popular needlecraft.

◆ ◆ ◆

Choosing the Right Crochet Hook

Crochet hooks, which are made of steel, aluminum, or wood, come in many sizes, each suited to a specific-size thread or yarn. The thicker the yarn, the bigger the hook you will need. It is helpful to have an assortment of sizes so you can adjust your gauge easily as you begin to follow pattern directions.

• The smallest hooks, used primarily with fine, lace-weight threads, are steel. The sizes are numbered from 00 through 14. The larger the number (Size 14, for example), the smaller the hook; and the lower the number, the larger the hook.

• Aluminum hooks are larger than steel hooks and are sized by letters. C is the smallest, K is the largest. Aluminum hooks are used more frequently than steel or wooden ones because they are suitable for working with most yarns.

• Wooden hooks—used with thick yarns—come in sizes Q, R, and S. If the yarn snags on the hook as you work, sandpaper the tip.

Matching Hooks to Yarns and Threads

Yarns and threads for crocheting are made from natural fibers, synthetics, and blends. When spun into different thicknesses or subjected to special treatments, they acquire their own characteristics of weight (or thickness) and texture.

• Yarns fall into approximately four groups, according to weight: sock or baby yarns, sport yarns, worsted yarns, and bulky yarns. As a general rule, use hooks C and D for slender sock or baby yarns; F and G for sport-weight yarns; G and H for worsted weights; and I through S for bulky yarns.

• Mercerized cotton threads also have their own weights, which are called sizes and are numbered 5, 10, 20, 30, 40, and 50. Pearl cottons are available in four sizes: 3, 5, 8, and 10. The smaller the number assigned to these threads, the heavier their weights. Use a Size 13 or 14 hook on Sizes 40 and 50 threads, an 11 or 12 hook on Size 30 threads, a 9 or 10 hook on Size 20 threads, and a 7 or 8 hook on Size 10 threads.

Bedspread cotton is not sized by number. Manufacturers usually specify hook size on the labels wrapped around the balls or skeins.

• When matching hooks to yarns, avoid confusing the number of plies of a yarn with the yarn's weight. A yarn spun with a single ply may be thick; a yarn spun with four plies may be thin. Select a hook appropriate for the thickness (or weight) of the yarn, not the number of plies.

Then, crochet a 4x4-inch swatch in the stitches indicated in the instructions to check your own gauge against the gauge recommended for the pattern.

Maintaining Tension and Gauge

Creating a consistently soft, firm fabric is every crocheter's goal. To do so, you will need to stitch with the correct tension and gauge.

• Tension is controlled by how tightly you grip the yarn as you work the crochet stitches. Gauge is normally determined by the hook size and is a term used to define the number of stitches per inch.

• Maintaining even tension keeps the shape and size of the stitches uniform. As you crochet, keep the following in mind: The thickest part of the hook, between the indentation where you rest your thumb and the point where the hook becomes narrower, governs the size of the loops. To keep stitches even, do not tighten or pull up on the thread as you slide each stitch over the end of the hook.

• When pattern instructions include a gauge notation, working to the gauge specified is important for the finished size of your project. Accurate gauge is obtained by experimenting with the hook size. For example, if a pattern calls for a gauge of 4 stitches per inch using a Size G hook, work a swatch using the recommended hook. You may find the tension you use for crocheting makes 11 stitches every 2 inches. To correct this discrepancy, either loosen your grip on the yarn or switch to a larger hook.

• When your work is too tight for a given gauge (too many stitches per inch), change to a larger-size hook. When the work is too loose, change to a smaller-size hook. As you gain experience you'll learn which hooks work best for you with different weights of yarn.

Stitching Tips and Techniques

• When working a chain, the loop on the hook never counts as a stitch. "Ch 50" means to work 50 chain stitches *plus* the slip knot and the loop on the hook.

• Turning chains always count as the first stitch of a new row or round, *except* when you single crochet. When working a straight edge in rows, work the turning chains as follows:

To begin a row of sc, ch 1, turn, and work the first sc in the first st.

To begin a new row of hdc, ch 2, turn, and work the first hdc in the second st. To begin a new row of dc, ch 3, turn, and work the first dc in the second st. To begin a new row of trc, ch 4, turn, and work the first trc in the second st.

The same rules apply for working in rounds, except when the instructions specify otherwise.

• When directions are not specific, always work under the *two top loops* of the stitches. Only crochet into front or back loops when instructions specify that you should.

• A dash (—) in a pattern is a reference point only. The information following the dash tells you how many stitches you have worked, *or* it names a special pattern stitch (such as a popcorn or shell). In the latter case, the pattern stitch will not be repeated in the directions. Refer to the information preceding the dash to repeat the pattern stitch when it is required.

• The words "end off," "fasten off," and "break off" are synonymous, and mean that you are finished working with the thread or yarn. Cut the thread, leaving a 4- to 6-inch tail, yarn over, and pull the strand through the loop on the hook. Weave the strand into the back of the finished work.

• If you think you are going to run out of yarn in the middle of a row, attach new yarn *before* beginning the row. Or, add yarn by *splicing* it. To splice, separate the plies along the last 4 inches of both the yarn you are working with and the new yarn. Overlap and twist together half the plies from the old and new yarns, holding the remaining plies out of the way. After twisting and joining plies, cut away the unused plies of both yarns. Continue crocheting with the new (joined) yarn.

• Before joining crocheted pieces, determine how you want the finished item (for example, a sweater or afghan) to lie.

To obtain a plain flat finish, with smooth seams, sew pieces together using whip or overcast stitches. For a decorative flat finish (also with smooth seams), whipstitch only in the *back* loops of the crochet stitches. Also, whipstitch bulky garment pieces together.

Using a large, blunt needle and the same thread or yarn used for the project, sew with the right sides of the pieces together. Whipstitch or overcast in every crochet stitch along the edges to be joined. Whipstitching in the back loops results in a firm joining; whipstitching under *both* strands of the stitches on both pieces results in a firmer joining. Avoid pulling the yarn or thread too tightly as you sew. The seam should have as much give as the crocheted work.

Backstitches are sometimes suitable for seams, but only when the work is thin, dense, and crocheted with a thin yarn or thread.

Instead of sewing seams, you may slip-stitch them together. A slip-stitched seam is smooth on the face of the crocheted fabric, but ridged on the underside. When using this technique, work with the right sides facing. Align the pieces and work in every crochet stitch under both strands of the two pieces being joined or in the back loops only. Use a hook one size larger than the hook used for the crocheted pieces to keep the joinings from being too taut.

To obtain a definite seam line or outline specific shapes, use single crochet stitches to join pieces. Hold the pieces with the *wrong* sides facing and work single crochet stitches in all the back loops of the two pieces. This technique will produce a ridge on the right side between the two pieces being joined.

• Symbols help to shorten directions. Asterisks (*) indicate pattern repeats within a row or round. Work the stitches following the * as many times as indicated, *in addition to* the first pattern repeat.

Parentheses, ( ), and brackets, [ ], indicate repetition. When a pattern reads, "[dc in next 3 sts, ch 2, (2 dc in next st) 3 times] 5 times," the directions within the parentheses are repeated three times and the entire sequence is repeated a total of five times.

Parentheses also indicate several stitches are worked as a unit in one stitch, loop, or space. If a pattern reads, "in next lp work (sc, 3 dc, sc)," all the stitches within the parentheses are worked *in the next lp.*

◆ ◆ ◆

Abbreviations and Stitch Diagrams

Abbreviations

beg	beginning
bl	block
ch	chain
cl	cluster
dc	double crochet
dec	decrease
dtr	double triple crochet
fol	following
grp	group
hdc	half double crochet
inc	increase
lp(s)	loop(s)
MC	Main Color
pat	pattern
pc	popcorn
rem	remaining
rep	repeat
rnd(s)	round(s)
sc	single crochet
sk	skip
sl st	slip stitch
sp	space
st(s)	stitch(es)
tog	together
trc	triple crochet
yo	wrap yarn over hook
*	repeat from * as indicated
( )	repeat between ( )s as indicated
[ ]	repeat between [ ]s as indicated

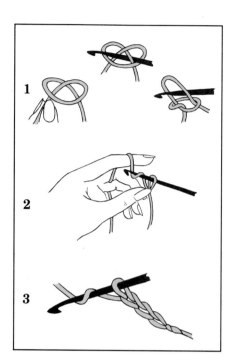

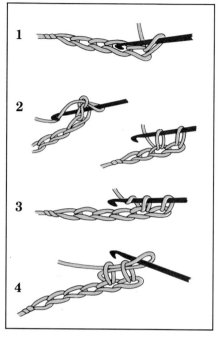

Chain Stitch

1 Start by making a slipknot on the hook about 6 inches from the yarn end. Pull one end of the yarn to tighten the knot.

2 Wrap yarn around the little finger of your left hand, and bring it up behind the next finger, under the middle finger, and back over the index finger. Hold the slipknot between your left thumb and middle finger. Hold the crochet hook between the right index finger and thumb, as you would a pencil.

3 Make a chain by wrapping the yarn over the hook and drawing it through the loop on the hook. Repeat step 3 to make a foundation chain.

Single Crochet

Chain 20.

1 Insert the crochet hook into the second chain from the hook, under the two upper strands of yarn.

2 Wrap yarn over the hook and draw yarn through the chain—2 lps rem on hook.

3 Wrap yarn over hook.

4 Draw yarn through the 2 lps on the hook—single crochet made. Rep steps 1-4 across the row, working sc in *next* ch and *each* of the following chs.

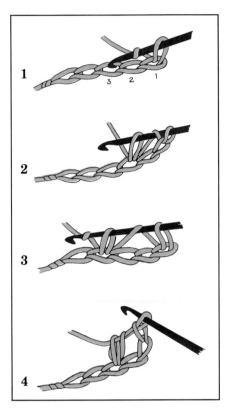

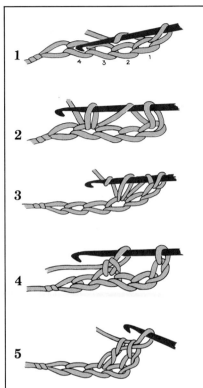

Slip Stitch

Chain 20.

1 Insert the crochet hook under the two top strands of the second chain from the crochet hook. Wrap yarn over the hook and with a single motion, pull the yarn through the chain and the loop on the hook—slip stitch made. Insert the hook under the two top strands of the next chain, then yarn over and draw the yarn through the chain and the loop on the hook.

2 Repeat this procedure to the end of the chain, or as specified. Slip stitch is used as a joining stitch when working in rnds, or to bind and strengthen edges.

Treble Crochet

Chain 20.

1 Wrap yarn over hook twice and insert hook into fifth chain, under two top strands of yarn.

2 Wrap yarn over hook and draw a loop through the chain—4 lps rem on hook.

3 Wrap yarn over hook, draw yarn through two loops on hook—3 lps rem on hook.

4 Wrap yarn over hook, draw through 2 lps on hook—2 lps rem on hook.

5 Wrap yarn over hook, draw through rem 2 lps on hook—triple crochet made. Rep steps 1-5, working trc in *next* ch and *each* ch across the row.

Half Double Crochet

Chain 20.

1 Wrap yarn over hook and insert hook into the third chain from the hook, under two upper strands of yarn.

2 Wrap yarn over the hook and draw a loop through the chain—3 lps rem on hook.

3 Wrap yarn over hook.

4 Draw yarn through the 3 lps on hook—half double crochet made. Rep steps 1-4 across the row, working hdc in *next* ch and *each* fol ch.

Double Crochet

Chain 20.

1 Wrap yarn over hook and insert hook into the fourth chain from the hook, under two upper strands of yarn.

2 Wrap yarn over the hook and draw a loop through the chain—3 lps rem on hook.

3 Wrap yarn over hook.

4 Draw yarn through two loops on hook—2 lps rem on hook.

5 Wrap yarn over hook and draw yarn through last two loops on hook—double crochet made. Rep steps 1-5 across the row, working dc in the *next* ch and *each* of the following chs.

LACY ACCENTS
for your home

Romantic and elegant, the crocheted
accessories in this section are just what you
need to add sparkle and freshness
to your home decor.

These pillows are so quick and simple
to stitch that even beginning crocheters can
make them with ease. A familiar
popcorn design is worked into a 15-inch-
square pillow, *far left*.
Add a second fabric ruffle and substitute
ribbon and fabric strips for the
crocheted border to make the
pillow below. Also in the cradle are square
and bolster-shape designs patterned
with filet crochet. For a closer look
at the curtain draped over the cradle,
please turn the page.

Instructions for all the projects in this
section begin on page 36.

♦ ♦ ♦

Either of these airy
needlework master-
pieces is sure to bring
a breath of spring to
a favorite spot in
your house. The cro-
cheted runner, *left,* is
assembled from ten
5½-inch squares, and
measures 13x32 inch-
es once the fanned
edging is added
around the border.

The curtains, *oppo-
site,* are stitched with
lattice-filled dia-
monds set into a filet
crochet background
to filter and soften
the sunlight. The pan-
els shown are 26x56
inches, but the pat-
tern includes instruc-
tions for adjusting
the size to your own
windows.

LACY
ACCENTS

◆ ◆ ◆

There's no nicer way to set an elegant table than with a beautiful handmade cloth. This magnificent design features rows and rows of pineapples—a popular crochet motif as well as a traditional symbol of joyous hospitality.

A spectacular spider web medallion forms the center of the cloth. The same spider web design, worked into a diamond pattern along the softly scalloped edge, turns this cloth into a masterful composition in crochet.

The finished cloth, worked in mercerized cotton, measures 72 inches in diameter.

◆ ◆ ◆
LACY
ACCENTS
◆ ◆ ◆

Crocheting a bed-spread is admittedly a challenge. But once you've completed one of these elegant patterns from Hyde Park, the historic home of Franklin Roosevelt, you should take great pride in your craftsmanship and in knowing that you've created an heirloom for future generations to enjoy.

The filet crochet bedspread, *below,* is bordered with a graceful sawtooth edging. Hexagonal motifs dotted with popcorns make up the coverlet, *opposite.*

Popcorn Pillow
Shown on page 28

Finished size of pillow is 15 inches square, excluding border.

MATERIALS
- Coats & Clark Royal Mouliné Knit and Crochet Thread: 2 (400-yard) balls white
- Size 7 steel crochet hook
- 16-inch knife-edge pillow form
- Fabric for pillow and ruffle

Abbreviations: See pages 26-27.

INSTRUCTIONS
Beg at center, ch 5. Join with sl st to form ring.

Rnd 1: Ch 3, work 2 dc in ring, (ch 3, work 3 dc in ring) 3 times; ch 1, hdc in top of ch-3 to form last lp.

Rnd 2: Ch 3, dc in lp just made, dc in top of ch-3, dc in back lp of next 2 dc; (in next lp make 2 dc, ch 3 and 2 dc; dc in back lp of next 3 dc) 3 times; 2 dc in same lp used at beg of rnd, ch 1, hdc in top of ch-3.

Rnd 3: Ch 3, dc in lp just made; dc in top of ch-3 and in back lp of next 2 dc; * **make 5 dc in back lp of next dc, drop lp from hook, insert hook from front to back in first dc of the 5-dc grp and draw dropped lp through, ch 1 to fasten—popcorn st (pc) made;** dc in back lp of next 3 dc; in next lp make 2 dc, ch 3 and 2 dc, dc in back lp of next 3 dc. Rep from * around, ending last rep with 2 dc in first lp used, ch 1, hdc in top of ch-3.

Rnd 4: Ch 3, dc in loop just made; dc in top of ch-3 and in back lp of next 2 dc, * (pc in back lp of next dc, dc in back lp of next 3 sts) twice; in next corner lp make 2 dc, ch 3 and 2 dc; dc in back lp of next 3 dc. Rep from * around, ending last rep with 2 dc in first lp used, ch 1, hdc in top of ch-3.

Note: Unless otherwise stated, beg and end each rnd as before. Always work into back lp of each st and count ch-3 at beg of rnds as a dc.

Rnd 5: Ch 3, dc in lp just made, dc in first 3 dc, * (pc st in next dc, dc in next 3 sts) 3 times; in next lp make 2 dc, ch 3 and 2 dc; dc in next 3 dc. Rep from * around, join as before.

Rnds 6-8: Same as Rnd 5 except on Rnd 6, rep between ( )'s 4 times; on Rnd 7, rep between ( )'s 5 times; on Rnd 8, rep between ( )'s 6 times. There will be 6 pc on each side at end of Rnd 8.

Rnd 9: Ch 3, dc in lp just made, * dc in next 7 sts, (pc in next dc, dc in next 3 sts) 4 times; pc in next dc, dc in next 7 sts; in next lp make 2 dc, ch 3 and 2 dc. Rep from * around, ending as before.

Rnd 10: Ch 3, dc in lp just made, * dc in next 11 dc, (pc in next dc, dc in next 3 sts) 3 times; pc in next dc, dc in next 11 sts; in next lp make 2 dc, ch 3 and 2 dc. Rep from * around, ending as before.

Rnd 11: Ch 3, dc in lp just made, * dc in next 15 dc, (pc in next dc, dc in next 3 sts) twice; pc in next dc, dc in next 15 sts; in next lp make 2 dc, ch 3 and 2 dc. Rep from * around, ending as before.

Rnd 12: Ch 3, dc in lp just made, * dc in next 19 dc, pc in next dc, dc in next 3 sts, pc in next dc, dc in next 19 sts; in next lp make 2 dc, ch 3 and 2 dc. Rep from * around, ending as before.

Rnd 13: Ch 3, dc in lp just made, * dc in next 23 dc, pc in next dc, dc in next 23 sts; in next lp make 2 dc, ch 3 and 2 dc. Rep from * around, ending as before.

Rnd 14: Ch 3, dc in lp just made, * dc in each st to next lp, in next lp make 2 dc, ch 3 and 2 dc. Rep from * around, ending as before.

Rnd 15: Ch 3, dc in lp just made, * (ch 1, sk next dc, dc in next 2 dc) across to next corner. In corner lp make 2 dc, ch 3, 2 dc. Rep from * around, ending as before.

Rnd 16: Ch 3, dc in lp just made, * dc in each dc and each ch to corner. In corner lp make 2 dc, ch 3 and 2 dc. Rep from * around, ending as before.

Rnd 17: Ch 3, dc in lp just made, * dc in next 3 dc, (pc in next dc, dc in next 3 dc) 15 times; in next lp make 2 dc, ch 3 and 2 dc. Rep from * around, ending as before.

Rnd 18: Ch 3, dc in lp just made, * dc in next 3 dc, (pc in next dc, dc in next 3 sts) 16 times; in next lp make 2 dc, ch 3 and 2 dc. Rep from * around, ending as before.

Rnd 19: Work as for Rnd 14.

- End here for pillow beneath cradle. Center crocheted piece atop 16-inch-square fabric; sew in place. Embellish edges with ribbons. Finish pillow and ruffling as indicated at end of instructions, except make two ruffles, one 2 inches wide and one 4 inches wide. Fold both strips in half, place raw edges together, and gather as one ruffle.

Rnd 20: Ch 4, dc in lp just made, * (ch 1, sk next dc, dc in next dc) across to next corner, ending ch 1, sk dc. In corner lp make (dc, ch 1, dc, ch 3, dc, ch 1, and dc). Rep from * around, ending with (dc, ch 1) twice and hdc in third ch of ch-4 in first corner lp at beg of rnd.

Rnd 21: Work as for Rnd 16.

Rnd 22: Ch 3, dc in lp just made, * (dc in next 3 dc, pc in next dc) 6 times; dc in next 37 dc; (pc in next dc, dc in next 3 dc) 6 times; in next lp make 2 dc, ch 3 and 2 dc. Rep from * around, ending as before.

Rnd 23-27: Ch 3, dc in lp just made, * (dc in next 3 dc, pc in next dc) 6 times; dc in each dc to next pc, dc in next pc, dc in next dc, (pc in next dc, dc in next 3 sts) 6 times; in next lp make 2 dc, ch 3 and 2 dc. Rep from * around, join as before.

Rnd 28: Work as for Rnd 14.

Rnd 29: Ch 4, dc in lp just made, * ch 1, dc in next dc, ** ch 1, sk next dc, dc in next dc. Rep from ** to corner; in next lp make (ch 1, dc) twice, ch 3, in same lp make dc, ch 1 and dc. Rep from * around, ending last rep with (dc, ch 1) twice in first lp used, hdc in third ch of ch-4. Fasten off.

Finishing: Cut two 16-inch fabric squares; cut a strip of fabric 4 yards long and 6 inches wide for ruffle; stitch short ends together. Fold strip in half with wrong sides together; run gathering stitch ½ inch from raw edge and gather to fit the fabric square. Sew ruffle in place (½-inch seams). With right sides facing, sew two squares together on three sides. Attach crochet piece to one side of pillow top. Insert pillow form; hand-sew fourth sides together.

Lacy Square Pillow
Shown on page 28

Finished size of pillow is 12 inches square, excluding the ruffle.

——————MATERIALS——————
- Coats & Clark Royal Mouliné knit and crochet thread: 1 (400-yard) ball white
- Size 4 steel crochet hook
- 12-inch square pillow form
- Fabric for covering pillow form

Abbreviations: See pages 26-27.

——————INSTRUCTIONS——————
Note: Post trc: Work trc around post of st from back to front to back.

Beg at center, ch 6; sl st to form ring.

Rnd 1: Ch 4 for first trc, 3 trc in ring, * ch 3, 4 trc in ring. Rep from * twice more, ending with ch 3, join to top of beg ch-4; turn.

Rnd 2: Sl st in next 2 ch, ch 4, turn; 2 trc in same corner sp, * post trc in next 4 trc; in next corner sp work 3 trc, ch 3, 3 trc. Rep from * twice more, ending with post trc in next 4 trc, 3 trc in corner sp, ch 3, join to top of beg ch-4; turn.

Rnds 3-8: Sl st in next 2 ch, ch 4, turn; 2 trc in same corner sp, * post trc in each trc to next corner, in corner sp work 3 trc, ch 3, 3 trc. Rep from * twice more, ending with post trc in each trc to corner, 3 trc in last corner sp, ch 3, join to top of beg ch—46 trc on each side of last rnd.

Rnd 9: Sc around post of trc (ch 4) below join, * sc around post of each trc to corner, ch 3 for corner. Rep from * around, join to first sc.

Rnd 10: Ch 4, trc in each of next 3 sc, * (ch 2, sk 2 sc, trc in each of next 4 sc) 7 times; ch 3 for corner, ** trc in each of next 4 sc. Rep from * three times more, ending last repeat at **; join to top of beg ch; turn.

Rnd 11: Sl st in next 3 ch, ch 4, turn; in same corner sp work 2 trc, ch 3, 3 trc; * trc in next trc, (ch 2, sk 2 trc, trc in next trc, 2 trc in ch-2 sp, trc in next trc) 7 times; ch 2, sk 2 trc, ** trc in next trc; in corner sp work 3 trc, ch 3, 3 trc, rep from * three times more, ending last repeat at **; join to top of beg ch-4.

Rnds 12-16: Sl st in next 2 trc (for Rnds 13-16, sl st in next 3 trc); ch 4, in corner sp work 3 trc, ch 3, 3 trc, * trc in next trc, (ch 2, sk 2 trc, trc in next trc, 2 trc in ch-sp, trc in next trc) 8 times; ch 2, sk 2 trc, ** trc in next trc; in corner work 3 trc, ch 3, 3 trc, rep from * three times more, ending the last repeat at **; join to top of beg ch.

Note: In Rnds 13-16, the number of times to rep between ( )s increases 1 more time for each rnd.

Rnd 17: Ch 3 for first dc, post dc in each of next 3 sts, * in corner sp work 4 dc, ch 2, 4 dc; (post dc in each of next 4 sts, 2 dc in ch-sp) to corner. Rep from * around, eliminating last corner on last rep; join to top of ch-3. Cut thread.

Rnd 18 (picot rnd): Join thread in any corner sp, ch 1, sc in same sp, **(ch 4, sc in second ch from hook) 3 times; ch 2, sc in same corner sp—picot corner made;** * sc in each of next 5 dc, (ch 4, sc in second ch from hook) 3 times; ch 2. Rep from * to next corner, work picot corner as before. Continue around rem 3 sides with pat as established; join and fasten off.

Finishing: See finishing instructions for Popcorn Pillow, opposite.

Bolster
Shown on page 28

Finished size of bolster is 15 inches long and 6 inches in diameter.

——————MATERIALS——————
- Coats & Clark Royal Mouliné knit and crochet thread: 2 (400-yard) balls white
- Size 4 steel crochet hook
- Bolster (or neck pillow) form—see finished size, above
- 1½ yards of ¾-inch-wide satin ribbon
- ½ yard of fabric for covering bolster

Abbreviations: See pages 26-27.

——————INSTRUCTIONS——————
Note: Post trc: Work trc around post of st from back to front to back.

Ch 86 to measure about 11 inches. *Row 1:* Trc in fifth ch from hook and in each of next 2 ch, * ch 2, sk 2 ch, trc in each of next 4 ch. Rep from * across—fourteen 4-trc grps; ch 6, turn.

Row 2: * Sk next 2 trc, trc in next trc, 2 trc in ch-2 sp, trc in next trc, ch 2; rep from * across, ending with trc in fourth ch of turning ch-6; turn. *Row 3:* * 2 trc in ch-2 sp, trc in next trc, ch 2, sk 2 trc, trc in next trc. Rep from * across, ending with 3 trc in turning ch-6 sp; ch 6, turn.

Rows 4-36: Rep Rows 2-3 alternately. Cut thread. Weave last row to edge of beg ch, forming a tube.

Bolster ends: *Rnd 1:* Join the thread at seam at one end of tube, ch 4 for first trc, * 2 trc over next trc post, 4 trc over next trc post. Rep from * around, ending with 3 trc over last post, join to top of beg ch.

Rnds 2-5: Ch 4 for first trc, post trc in each trc around; join.

Rnd 6: Ch 1, work sc around each trc post; join to top of first sc.

Rnd 7: Ch 4 for first trc, trc in next sc, * ch 1, sk sc, trc in each of next 2 sc. Rep from * around, end ch 1; join to top of beg ch.

Rnds 8-9: Ch 4 for first trc, trc in next trc, * ch 1, trc in each of next 2 trc. Rep from * around, end ch 1; join to top of beg ch.

Rnd 10: Sl st to next ch-1 sp, ch 6, * trc in next ch-sp, ch 2. Rep from * around; join to fourth ch of beg ch-6. *Rnds 11-12:* Ch 6, * trc in next trc, ch 2. Rep from * around; join to fourth ch of beg ch-6.

Rnd 13: Sl st in ch-sp, ch 4, trc in same sp, * ch 1, 2 trc in next sp. Rep from * around; ch 1, join to top of beg ch. *Rnd 14:* Ch 4, trc in next trc, * ch 1, trc in next 2 trc. Rep from * around, ending with ch 1; join to top of beg ch.

Rnd 15 (picot rnd): * **(Ch 4, sc in second ch from hook) 3 times; ch 2, sc in next trc—picot lp made;** sc in ch-sp, sc in next 2 trc, sc in ch-sp, sc in next trc. Rep from * around; join. Fasten off. Work the other end of bolster to correspond.

Finishing: Cover bolster with fabric. Place the covered pillow inside the crocheted cover. Weave ribbon through the ch-sps at each end of the bolster ends (on Rnd 11). Draw ribbon together, gathering ends, and tie securely.

37

Table Runner

Shown on page 30

Finished runner is 13x32 inches.

MATERIALS
- DMC Cébélia crochet cotton, Size 10: 3 (50-gram) balls of white
- Size 8 steel crochet hook

Abbreviations: See pages 26-27.

INSTRUCTIONS

First strip—first motif: Ch 8; join with sl st to form ring.

Rnd 1: Ch 3, work 23 dc in ring; join with sl st to top of beg ch-3—24 dc, counting beg ch-3 as dc.

Rnd 2: Ch 7, dc in same sp as joining, * ch 2, sk 2 dc, dc in next dc, ch 2, sk 2 dc, in next dc work dc, ch 4, dc. Rep from * twice more, ch 2, sk 2 dc, dc in next dc, ch 2; join to third ch of beg ch-7; sl st into ch-4 sp—square motif established.

Rnd 3: Ch 4, in same sp work 4 trc, ch 4, 5 trc, * ch 2, sk dc, trc in next dc, ch 2, in next ch-4 sp work 5 trc, ch 4, 5 trc. Rep from * twice more; ch 2, sk dc, trc in next dc, ch 2; join to top of beg ch-4.

Rnd 4: **Ch 3, holding back on hook the last lp of each trc, trc in each of next 4 trc, yo, draw through rem 5 lps on hook, ch 1 for eye of cluster—first trc cluster (cl) made;** * ch 2, in next ch-4 sp work 5 trc, ch 4, 5 trc; ch 2, **holding back on hook last lp of each trc, trc in next 5 trc, yo, draw through rem 6 lps on hook, ch 1 for eye of cl—5-trc cl made;** ch 2, *in next trc work* **trc, ch 2, trc—V-st made;** ch 2, work 5-trc cl over next 5 trc. Rep from * twice more; ch 2, in next ch-4 sp work (5 trc, ch 4, 5 trc), ch 2, 5-trc cl over next 5 trc, ch 2, V-st in next trc, ch 2; join with sl st in eye of first cl.

Rnd 5: Sl st in each of next 2 ch and next trc, ch 3, work a first trc cl over next 4 trc, * ch 2, in next ch-4 sp work (5 trc, ch 4, 5 trc), ch 2, work a 5-trc cl over next 5 trc, ch 4, in ch-2 sp of V-st work (trc, ch 2) 3 times; trc in same sp; ch 4, ** 5-trc cl over next 5 trc. Rep from * 3 times, ending last rep at **; join ch-4 to eye of first cl.

Rnd 6: Sl st in each of next 2 ch and next trc, ch 3, work a first trc cl over next 4 trc, * ch 2, in next ch-4 sp work (5 trc, ch 4, 5 trc), ch 2, work 5-trc cl over next 5 trc, ch 4, (V-st in ch-2 sp of next V-st, ch 2) twice; V-st in next ch-2 sp—5 ch-2 sps made; ch 4, ** trc cl over next 5 trc. Rep from * 3 times, ending last rep at **; join ch-4 to eye of first cl.

Rnd 7: Sl st in each of next 2 ch and next trc, ch 3, work a first trc cl over next 4 trc, * ch 4, 5 trc in ch-4 sp, ch 4, trc cl over next 5 trc, ch 4, sk next trc cl, (V-st in next ch-2 sp, ch 2) 4 times; V-st in next ch-2 sp— 9 ch-2 sps; ch 4, ** trc cl over next 5 trc. Rep from * 3 times more, ending last rep at **; join ch-4 to eye of first cl.

Rnd 8: Ch 1, sc in same st as joining, * ch 10, trc cl over next 5 trc, ch 6, sl st in ch just before eye of trc cl just made, ch 10, sc in eye of next trc cl, ch 6, sc in next ch-2 sp, (ch 4, sc in next ch-2 sp) 8 times; ch 6, ** sc in eye of next cl. Rep from * 3 times more, end last rep at **; join ch-6 to sc at beg of rnd. Fasten off.

First strip—second motif: Crochet same as for first motif through Rnd 7, and work Rnd 8 until instructions through the set of *s have been worked once.

To join motifs: * Ch 10, trc cl over next 5 trc, ch 3; drop lp from hook, insert hook through ch-6 corner lp of first motif, pull dropped lp through, ch 3, sl st in ch just before eye of trc cl made on second motif, ch 5; drop lp from hook; insert hook under ch-10 lp of first motif, pull dropped lp through, ch 5, sc in eye of next trc cl; ch 3; drop lp from hook, insert hook under ch-6 lp of first motif, pull dropped lp through; ch 3, sc in ch-2 sp of V-st of second motif, (ch 2; drop lp from hook, insert hook under corresponding ch-4 lp of first motif, pull dropped lp

through, ch 2, sc in next ch-2 sp of second motif) 8 times; ch 3; drop lp from hook, insert hook under ch-6 lp of first motif, pull dropped lp through, ch 3, sc in eye of next trc cl, ch 5; drop lp from hook, insert hook under ch-10 lp of first motif, pull dropped lp through, ch 5, trc cl over next 5 trc, ch 3; drop lp from hook, insert hook through ch-6 corner lp of first motif, pull dropped lp through, ch 3, sl st in ch just before eye of trc cl made on second motif; complete second motif as for first motif, with no more joinings.

First strip—third, fourth, and fifth motifs: Work each motif in same manner as second motif.

Second strip—first motif: Crochet as for first strip, second motif; join to first motif of first strip.

Second strip—second, third, fourth, and fifth motifs: Work as for second, third, fourth, and fifth motifs of first strip.

Note: These 4 motifs are worked as for those on first strip except they have joinings on 2 sides: 1 side joins to the first strip and 1 side joins to the second strip. Continue to join as before for second motif on first strip.

In corner where motif joins both strips, work first side of joining through the trc cl, then: ch 3, drop lp from hook, insert hook through ch-6 corner lp of first strip, second motif, pull the dropped lp through; drop lp from the hook, insert hook through ch-6 corner lp on second strip, first motif; pull dropped lp through, ch 3, sl st in ch just before eye of the trc cl made on motif in progress.

Continue joinings along the third side, as established, and work fourth side with no more joinings.

Edging: *Rnd 1:* Join thread in next ch-6 corner lp; * ch 6, trc in same lp, (ch 2, trc in same lp) twice—4 trc and 3 ch-2 sps in corner ch-6 lp, counting beg ch-6 as trc and ch-2 sp; [ch 6, sc in ch-10 lp, ch 6, sc in ch-6 lp, (ch 5, sc in next ch-4 lp) 8 times; ch 5, sc in ch-6 lp, ch 6, sc in ch-10 lp, ch 6, sc in center of joining between ch-6 lps of next 2 motifs.] Rep bet [ ]s once more, ending with sc in corner ch-6 lp. Rep from * to next corner ch-6 lp and at the same time, rep bet [ ]s 4 times more along the long side of the runner. Beg at * work next 2 sides as given for first 2 sides. Complete rnd with ch-3, trc in fourth ch of ch-6 at beg of rnd.

Rnd 2: Ch 5, sc in next ch-2 sp, [ch 5, in next ch-2 lp work (trc, ch 2, trc); ch 5, sc in next ch-2 lp], * ch 5, sc in next lp. Rep from * to next ch-6 corner lp. Rep bet [ ]s for corner. Rep from * to next ch-6 corner lp. Work as established to complete rnd, ending with ch 2, dc in trc at end of Rnd 1.

Rnd 3: (Ch 6, sc in next lp) twice; * [ch 6, in corner ch-2 sp work (trc, ch 2, trc), (ch 6, sc in next lp) 12 times; (ch 2, dc in next lp) 5 times], (ch 6, sc in next lp) 12 times. Rep bet [ ]s once more; ** (ch 6, sc in next lp) 8 times; (ch 2, dc in next lp) 5 times. Rep from ** twice more; *** (ch 6, sc in next lp) 12 times. Rep from * up to *** once more, ending rnd with (ch 6, sc in next lp) 9 times; ch 3, trc in dc at end of Rnd 2.

Rnd 4: (Ch 6, **sl st in third ch from hook—picot made;** ch 3, sc in next lp) 3 times; * ch 6, picot, ch

3; in ch-2 corner sp work (trc, ch 5, picot, ch 2, trc), (ch 6, picot, ch 3, sc in next lp) 13 times; (ch 1, dc in next ch-2 lp) 4 times; ch 1, sc in next lp, (ch 6, picot, ch 3, sc in next lp) 12 times; ch 6, picot, ch 3; in ch-2 corner sp work (trc, ch 5, picot, ch 2, trc); (ch 6, picot, ch 3, sc in next lp) 13 times; [(ch 1, dc in next ch-2 lp) 4 times; ch 1, sc in next lp; (ch 6, picot, ch 3, sc in next lp) 8 times.] Rep bet [ ]s twice more; ** (ch 6, picot, ch 3, sc in next lp) 12 times. Rep from * to ** once more, ending rnd with (ch 6, picot, ch 3, sc in next lp) 8 times; ch 6, picot, ch 3, sl st in trc at end of Rnd 3. Fasten off.

Block runner and press.

Filet Crochet Curtain Panels
Shown on page 31

The finished size of each panel is 56 inches long and 26 inches wide. To adjust the length of the panels to fit your windows, see instructions below.

MATERIALS
For two panels
· DMC Cébélia crochet cotton, Size 10: 13 (50-gram) balls of white
· Size 8 steel crochet hook, or size to obtain gauge
· 2 yards of 1½-inch-wide grosgrain ribbon

Abbreviations: See pages 26-27.
Gauge: 7 horizontal sps = 2 inches; 8 vertical sps = 2 inches.

INSTRUCTIONS
Note on filet crochet: Each shaded square on the chart, *below*, represents 1 block (bl). A single bl is 4 dc wide; adjacent bls are 3 dc wide. (For example, 2 adjacent blocks would be 7 dc wide; 3 adjacent blocks would be 10 dc wide.) Ch-3 at the beg of each row counts as 1 dc.

Each open square on the chart represents 1 space (sp). A single sp is (dc, ch 2, sk 2 sts, dc in next st). Adjacent sps are (ch 2, sk 2 sts, dc in next st).

continued

Bottom edge

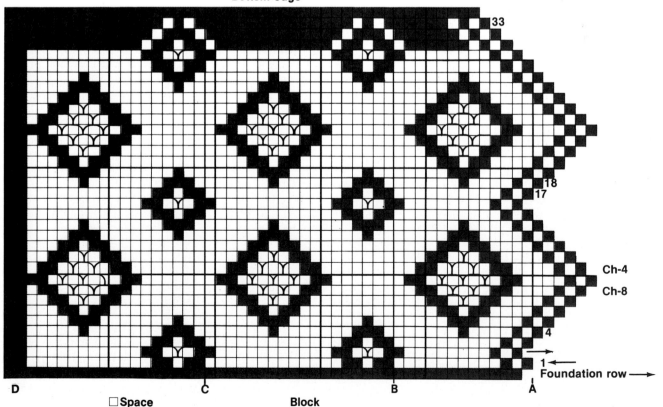

33

18
17

Ch-4

Ch-8

4

1

Foundation row →

D   C   B   A

□ Space   ■ Block

39

The curved lines in the center of the diamond pattern represent lacet stitches. The first lacet begins with a dc (the last dc of a bl), ch 5, sk 2 sts, dc in next st (the first dc of a bl). In the next row the design continues with two ch-5 lps and is worked as follows: Dc, ch 5, sc in ch-5 lp, ch 5, sk 3 sts, dc in next st. Each additional row is worked in the same manner, inc or dec the number of ch-5 lps and sc's as indicated on the chart *(page 39)*.

Curtains—*foundation row:* Beg at top edge, ch 257, dc in fourth ch and in each ch across; ch 3, turn—255 dc.

Next 3 rows: Dc in each dc across; ch 3, turn. Now begin to work from chart, *page 39.*

Row 1 and all odd-numbered rows: Work across row from A to C, (work from B to C) twice; work from C to D to complete row.

Row 2 and all even-numbered rows: Work across from D to B, (work from C to B) twice; work from B to A to complete row. To adjust width of curtain, add or subtract number of repeats in center.

For length of curtain, work first 17 rows as given below. Rep Rows 4-17 thirteen times more, or for length desired less 4½ inches. Be sure to work through the complete set of pattern rows. Finish the lower edge (Rows 18-33) according to the chart.

Final row: * Dc in next 4 dc, ch 3, rep from * across. Fasten off.

Finishing: Sew grosgrain ribbon along the top edge of the curtain, along lines of first row of dc. Slide the curtain rod under the ribbon and stitch the ribbon in place, allowing for ease around the rod.

Filet crochet pattern (Rows 1-17): *Row 1:* 3 dc in first dc, ch 2, sk 2 dc, dc in next 4 dc, (ch 2, sk 2 dc, dc in next dc) 10 times—10 sps; [dc in next 6 dc, ch 5, sk 2 dc, dc in next 7 dc, (ch 2, sk 2 dc, dc in next dc) 13 times—13 sps]. Rep bet [ ]s twice more, or for required number of reps; dc in next 6 dc, ch 5, sk 2 dc, dc in next 7 dc, (ch 2, sk 2 dc, dc in next

dc) 12 times—12 sps; dc in next 4 dc and in top of turning ch; ch 3, turn.

Row 2: Sk first dc, dc in next 5 dc; refer to chart and work as follows: 11 sps, (2 bls, ch 5, sc in ch-5 lp, ch 5, 2 bls, 11 sps) 3 times; 2 bls, ch 5, sc in ch-5 lp, ch 5, 2 bls, 8 sps, 1 bl, 1 sp, 1 bl; ch 8, turn.

Row 3: **Dc in the sixth, seventh, and eighth ch from hook and first dc—bl made;** 1 sp, 1 bl, 10 sps; (2 bls—work 3 dc of second bl in ch-5 lp; ch 2, 2 bls—work 3 dc of first bl in ch-5 lp; 13 sps) 3 times; 2 bls, ch 2, 2 bls, 12 sps, 5 dc; ch 3, turn.

Row 4: 5 dc, 5 sps, (1 bl, 7 sps, 3 bls, 7 sps) 4 times; 1 bl, 4 sps, 1 bl, 1 sp, 1 bl; work 3 dc in turning ch-sp; ch 8, turn.

Row 5: Dc in sixth, seventh, and eighth ch from hook and first dc; 1 sp, 1 bl, 4 sps, (3 bls, 7 sps, 1 bl, 7 sps) 4 times; 3 bls, 4 sps, 5 dc; ch 3, turn.

Row 6: 5 dc, 3 sps, 2 bls, ch 5, 2 bls; (13 sps, 2 bls, ch 5, 2 bls) 4 times; 4 sps, 1 bl, 1 sp, 1 bl with 3 dc in turning ch-sp; ch 8, turn.

Row 7: Dc in sixth, seventh, and eighth ch from hook and in first dc; 1 sp, 1 bl, 4 sps, (2 bls, ch 5, sc in ch-5 lp, ch 5, 2 bls, 11 sps) 4 times; 2 bls, ch 5, sc, ch 5, 2 bls, 2 sps, 5 dc; ch 3, turn.

Row 8: 5 dc, 1 sp, [2 bls, (ch 5, sc in next ch-5 lp) twice; ch 5, 2 bls, 9 sps] 4 times; 2 bls, (ch 5, sc in next ch-5 lp) twice; ch 5, 2 bls, 4 sps, 1 bl, 1 sp, 1 bl; ch 3, turn.

Row 9: 3 dc in first dc, 1 sp, 1 bl, 4 sps, [2 bls, (ch 5, sc in next ch-5 lp) 3 times; ch 5, 2 bls, 7 sps] 4 times; 2 bls, (ch 5, sc in next ch-5 lp) 3 times; ch 5, 2 bls, 5 dc; ch 3, turn.

Row 10: 5 dc, 1 sp, [2 bls—work 3 dc of second bl in ch-5 lp, (ch 5, sc in next ch-5 lp) twice; ch 5, 2 bls—work 3 dc of first bl in ch-5 lp, 9 sps] 4 times; 2 bls, (ch 5, sc in next ch-5 lp) twice; ch 5, 2 bls, 4 sps, 1 bl, 1 sp, 1 bl; ch 4, turn.

Row 11: Sk next 2 dc, dc in next dc, 1 sp, 1 bl, 4 sps, (2 bls, ch 5, sc in ch-5 lp, ch 5, 2 bls, 11 sps) 4 times; 2 bls, ch 5, sc in ch-5 lp, ch 5; 2 bls, 2

sps, 5 dc; ch 3, turn.

Row 12: 5 dc, 3 sps, (2 bls, ch 2, 2 bls, 13 sps) 4 times; 2 bls, ch 2, 2 bls, 4 sps, 1 bl, 1 sp, 1 bl; ch 4, turn.

Row 13: Sk next 2 d, dc in next dc, 1 sp, 1 bl, 4 sps, (3 bls, 7 sps, 1 bl, 7 sps) 4 times; 3 bls, 4 sps, 5 dc; ch 3, turn.

Row 14: 5 dc, 5 sps, 1 bl, (7 sps, 3 bls, 7 sps, 1 bl) 4 times; 4 sps, 1 bl, 1 sp, 1 bl; ch 4, turn.

Row 15: Dc in fourth dc to beg first bl, 1 sp, 1 bl, 10 sps, (2 bls, ch 5, 2 bls, 13 sps) 3 times; 2 bls, ch 5, 2 bls, 12 sps, 5 dc; ch 3, turn.

Row 16: 5 dc, (11 sps, 2 bls, ch 5, sc in ch-5 lp, ch 5, 2 bl) 4 times; 8 sps, 1 bl, 1 sp, 1 bl; ch 8, turn.

Row 17: Dc in sixth, seventh, and eighth ch from hook and first dc; 1 sp, 1 bl, 10 sps, (2 bls, ch 2, 2 bls, 13 sps) 3 times; 2 bls, ch 2, 2 bls, 12 sps, 5 dc; ch 3, turn.

Pineapple Tablecloth
Shown on page 32-33

Finished cloth is approximately 72 inches in diameter.

——————**MATERIALS**——————
- J & P Coats mercerized thread, Size 20: 19 (300-yard) balls of ecru
- Size 7 steel crochet hook

Abbreviations: See pages 26-27.

——————**INSTRUCTIONS**——————
Ch 5, join with sl st to form a ring. *Rnd 1:* Ch 11, trc in ring, * ch 7, trc in ring. Rep from * 3 times more; ch 7, sl st in fourth ch of ch-11 at beg of rnd—6 ch-lps.

Rnd 2: Sl st in next 3 ch, ch 11, trc in same lp as sl sts, * ch 7 (trc, ch 7, trc) all in next ch-7 lp. Rep from * around, ending with ch 7, sl st in fourth ch of beg ch-11—12 lps.

Rnd 3: Sl st in next 5 ch, ch 4, 3 trc in same lp as sl sts, * ch 2 (4 trc, ch 7, 4 trc) in next ch-7 lp. Rep from * around, ending with ch 2, 4 trc in same lp as first 3 trc of rnd, ch 7, sl st in top of ch-4 at beg of rnd.

st in top of ch 4 at beg of rnd.

Rnd 4: Sl st in next 3 trc, ch 4, * (3 trc, ch 2, 3 trc) in ch-2 sp, trc in next trc, ch 3, sk 3 trc, sc in ch-7 lp, ch 3, sk 3 trc, trc in next trc. Rep from * around, ending last rep with ch 3, sl st in top of ch-4.

Rnd 5: Sl st in next 3 trc, ch 4, * 2 trc in ch-2 sp, trc in next trc, ch 6, sk 3 trc, sc over end of next ch-lp, sc in sc, sc in next ch-lp, ch 6, sk 3 trc, trc in next trc. Rep from * around, ending with ch 6, sl st in top of ch-4.

Rnd 6: Sl st in next 3 trc, ch 4, * 3 trc in ch-6 lp, ch 6, sc in center st of sc grp, ch 6, 3 trc over end of ch lp, trc in next trc, ch 7, sk 2 trc, trc in next trc. Rep from * around, ending with ch 7, sl st in top of ch-4.

Rnd 7: Sl st in next 3 trc, ch 4, * 3 trc in ch-lp, ch 2, 3 trc over end of next ch-lp, trc in next trc, ch 6, sk 3 trc, sc in ch-lp, ch 6, sk 3 trc, trc in next trc. Rep from * around, ending as for Rnd 5.

Rnds 8-10: Rep Rnds 5-7.

Rnd 11: Rep Rnd 5, except *ch 9 instead of ch 6.*

Rnd 12: Sl st across 3 trc, ch 4, * 3 trc in next lp, ch 7, sc in center sc, ch 7, 3 trc in next lp, trc in next trc, ch 4, sk 2 trc, trc in next trc. Rep from * around, ending with ch 4, sk 2 trc, join to top of ch-4.

Rnd 13: Sl st in next 3 trc, ch 4, * 3 trc in next ch-lp, ch 4, 3 trc over end of next ch-lp, trc in next trc, ch 6, sk 2 trc, trc in next trc, 2 trc in sp, trc in next trc, ch 6, sk 2 trc, trc in next trc. Rep from * around, ending with ch 6, sl st in top of beg ch-4.

Rnd 14: Sl st in next 3 trc, ch 4, * 2 trc in sp, trc in trc, ch 10, sk 3 trc, trc in next 4 trc, ch 10, sk 3 trc, trc in next trc. Rep from * around, ending with ch 10, sl st in top of ch-4.

Rnd 15: Ch 4, trc in each of rem trc on same grp, * ch 12, sk ch-lp, trc in each trc on next grp. Rep from * around, ending with ch 12, sl st in top of beg ch-4.

Rnd 16: Ch 4, trc in same st as sl st, * trc in each of rem trc in same grp, trc in same st as last trc made, ch 12, sk ch-lp, 2 trc in next trc. Rep

from * around, ending as before.

Rnds 17-18: Rep Rnds 15 and 16. End of Rnd 18—8 trc in group.

Rnd 19: Ch 4, trc in next 3 trc, * ch 7, trc in next 4 trc, ch 10, trc in next 4 trc. Rep from * around, ending as for Rnd 14.

Rnd 20: Ch 4, trc in next 3 trc, * ch 4, 4 trc in center st of ch-7 lp, ch 4, trc in next 4 trc, ch 8, trc in next 4 trc. Rep from * around, ending with ch 8, sl st in top of ch-4.

Rnd 21: Ch 4, trc in next 3 trc, * ch 4, 2 trc in each of next 4 trc, ch 4, trc in next 4 trc, ch 6, trc in next 4 trc. Rep from * around, ending as for Rnd 5.

Rnd 22: Ch 4, trc in next 3 trc. * ch 4, (2 trc in next trc, trc in next trc) 4 times; ch 4, trc in next 4 trc, ch 3, trc in next 4 trc. Rep from * around, ending with ch 3, sl st in top of ch-4.

Rnd 23: Ch 4, trc in next 3 trc, * ch 6, trc in next trc, (ch 4, trc in trc) 11 times; ch 6, trc in next 4 trc, sk lp, trc in next 4 trc. Rep from * around; end with sl st to top ch-4.

Rnd 24: Ch 3, trc in next trc; work a **joined trc over next 2 trc as follows: [yo hook twice, draw up a lp in next st, (yo, draw through 2 lps on hook) twice]; rep between [ ]s 1 more time, yo, draw through rem 3 lps on hook.** * Ch 6, sk ch-6 lp, sc in next ch-lp; in each ch-4 lp of pineapple work ch-4 and sc; ch 6, sk ch-6 lp, (work a joined trc over next 2 trc) 4 times. Rep from * around, ending with ch 6, (joined trc over 2 trc) twice, sl st in top of first trc of rnd.

Rnd 25: Ch 4, trc in next st, * ch 6, sk ch-6 lp, sc in next ch-lp; in each ch-4 lp of pineapple work ch 4 and sc; ch 6, sk ch-6 lp, trc in next 4 sts. Rep from * around, ending with ch 6, trc in each of 2 sts, sl st in top of ch-4.

Rnds 26-27: Rep Rnd 25.

Rnd 28: Ch 4, trc in same st as sl st, 2 trc in next trc, * ch 8, sk ch-6 lp,

sc in next ch-lp (ch 4, sc) in 6 ch-lps of pineapple, ch 8, 2 trc in each of next 4 trc. Rep from * around, ending with ch 8, 2 trc in each of next 2 trc, sl st in top of ch-4.

Rnd 29: Ch 4, trc in next 3 trc, * ch 8, sk lp, sc in next ch-lp, (ch 4, sc) in 5 ch-lps of pineapple, ch 8, trc in next 4 trc, ch 7, trc in next 4 trc. Rep from * around, end as Rnd 6.

Rnd 30: Ch 4, trc in next 3 trc, * ch 8, sk lp, sc in next ch-lp (ch 4, sc) in 4 ch-lps, ch 8, trc in next 4 trc, ch 4, 4 trc in center st of ch-7 lp, ch 4, trc in next 4 trc. Rep from * around, ending with ch 4, sl st in top ch-4.

Rnd 31: Ch 4, trc in next 3 trc, * ch 8, sk lp, sc in next ch-lp, (ch 4, sc) in next 3 ch-lps, ch 8, trc in next 4 trc, ch 4, 2 trc in each of next 4 trc, ch 4, trc in next 4 trc. Rep from * around, ending as before.

Rnd 32: Ch 4, trc in 3 trc, * ch 8, sk lp, sc in next ch-lp (ch 4, sc) in 2 ch-lps, ch 8, trc in next 4 trc, ch 4, 2 trc in each of next 2 trc, trc in all except final 2 trc of same grp, 2 trc in each of 2 trc, ch 4, trc in next 4 trc. Rep from * around, ending as before.

Rnd 33: Ch 4, trc in 3 trc, * ch 8, sk lp, sc in next ch-lp, ch 4, sc in next ch-lp, ch 8, trc in next 4 trc, ch 4, sk next lp (trc, ch 4) in each trc of next trc-grp, trc in next 4 trc. Rep from * around, ending as before.

Rnd 34: Ch 4, trc in 3 trc, * ch 8, sk lp, sc in next ch-lp, ch 8, trc in next 4 trc, ch 6, sk lp, sc in next ch-lp, (ch 4, sc) in 10 ch-lps; ch 6, trc in next 4 trc. Rep from * around, ending as for Rnd 5.

Rnd 35: Ch 4, trc in next 3 trc, * sk 2 ch-lps, trc in next 4 trc, ch 6, sk lp, sc in next ch-lp, (ch 4, sc) in 9 ch-lps, ch 6, trc in next 4 trc. Rep from * around, ending as before.

Rnd 36: Sl st in next 4 trc; rep as for Rnd 24.

Rnd 37: Rep Rnd 25.

Rnds 38-42: Rep Rnds 28-32.

Rnd 43: Rep Rnd 32, having 1 ch-4 lp in each pineapple.

Rnd 44: Ch 4, trc in 3 trc, * ch 8, sk ch-8 lp, sc in ch-4 lp, ch 8, trc in next 4 trc, (ch 4, trc in next trc) 16 times; ch 4, trc in next 4 trc; rep from * around, end as before.

continued

Rnd 45: Rep Rnd 35—14 ch-4 lps.

Rnd 46: Sl st in next 4 trc. Rep Rnd 24—13 ch-4 lps.

Rnd 47: Rep Rnd 25—12 ch-4 lps.

Rnd 48: Rep Rnd 28—11 ch-4 lps.

Rnd 49: Rep Rnd 29—10 ch-4 lps.

Rnd 50: Rep Rnd 30—9 ch-4 lps.

Rnd 51: Rep Rnd 31—8 ch-4 lps.

Rnd 52: Rep Rnd 32—7 ch-4 lps and 12 trc.

Rnd 53: Rep Rnd 32—6 ch-4 lps and 16 trc.

Rnd 54: Ch 4, trc in 3 trc; * ch 8, sk ch-8 lp, sc in next lp, (ch 4, sc in next lp) 5 times; ch 8, trc in next 4 trc, ch 4, (trc in next trc, ch 4) 16 times, trc in 4 trc; rep from * around, end as before.

Rnd 55: Ch 4, trc in 3 trc, * ch 8, sk lp, sc in next ch-lp, (ch 4, sc in next lp) 4 times; ch 8, trc in 4 trc, ch 6, sk ch-lp, sc in next lp, (ch 4, sc in next lp) 14 times; ch 6, trc in next 4 trc. Rep from * around; end same as Rnd 5.

Rnd 56: Rep Rnd 55—3 ch-4 lps and 13 ch-4 lps.

Rnd 57: Rep Rnd 55—2 ch-4 lps and 12 ch-4 lps.

Rnd 58: Rep Row 55—1 ch-4 lp and 11 ch-4 lps.

Rnd 59: Ch 4, trc in 3 trc, * ch 8, sk lp, sc in ch-4 lp, ch 8, sk lp, trc in 4 trc, ch 8, sk lp, sc in next lp, (ch 4, sc in next lp) 10 times; ch 8, sk ch lp, trc in 4 trc. Rep from * around.

Rnd 60: Rep Rnd 35.

Rnd 61: Sl st in the next 4 trc. Rep Rnd 24—8 ch-4 lps.

Rnd 62: Rep Rnd 25—7 ch-4 lps.

Rnd 63: Rep Rnd 28.

Rnd 64: Rep Rnd 29.

Rnd 65: Rep Rnd 30.

Rnd 66: Rep Rnd 31.

Rnd 67: Rep Rnd 32.

Rnd 68: Rep Rnd 32—1 ch-4 lp and 16 trc.

Rnd 69: Ch 4, trc in 3 trc, * ch 8, sk lp, sc in next ch-lp, ch 8, trc in 4 trc, ch 4, sk ch-lp, trc in next trc, (ch 4, trc in next trc) 15 times; ch 4, trc in next 4 trc. Rep from * around, ending with ch 4; join to top of ch-4.

Rnd 70: Ch 4, trc in 3 trc, * ch 7, sk 2 ch-lps, trc in next 4 trc, ch 6, sk lp, sc in next lp (ch 4, sc in next lp) 14 times; ch 6, trc in 4 trc. Rep from * around, ending as before.

Rnd 71: Ch 4, trc in 3 trc, * sc in ch-7 lp, sk trc, trc in next 3 trc, ch 6, sk lp, sc in next ch-lp, (ch 4, sc in next lp) 13 times; ch 6, sk lp, trc in next 4 trc. Rep from * around, end as last rnd.

Rnd 72: Sl st in next 4 sts; rep Rnd 24.

Rnds 73-74: Rep Rnd 25.

Rnd 75: Sl st in next trc, ch 4, * 3 trc in next ch-lp, ch 8, sc in next ch lp, (ch 4, sc) in 9 ch-lps; ch 8, 3 trc over end of next ch-lp, trc in next trc, ch 7, sk 2 trc, trc in next trc. Rep from * around; end with ch 7, sl st in top of ch-4.

Rnd 76: Sl st in next 3 trc, ch 4, * 3 trc in ch-lp, ch 8, sc in next lp, (ch 4, sc) in 8 ch-lps; ch 8, 3 trc over end of next ch-lp, trc in next trc, ch 6, sk 3 trc, sc in ch-7 lp, ch 6, sk 3 trc, trc in next trc; rep from * around; end with ch 6, sl st in top of ch-4.

Rnd 77: Sl st in next 3 trc, ch 4, * 3 trc in next ch-lp, ch 8, sc in next lp, (ch 4, sc) in 7 ch-lps, ch 8, 3 trc over end of ch-8 lp, trc in next trc, ch 6, sc over end of next lp, sc in sc, sc in next lp, ch 6, sk 3 trc, trc in next trc; rep from * around, end as last rnd.

Rnd 78: Sl st in 3 trc, ch 4, * 3 trc in next ch-lp, ch 8, sc in next lp, (ch 4, sc) in 6 ch-lps, ch 8, 3 trc over end of ch-8 lp, trc in next trc, ch 6, sc over end of next ch-lp, sc in next 3 sc, sc in next ch-lp, ch 6, sk 3 trc, trc in next trc. Rep from * around, end as last rnd.

Rnd 79: Sl st in next 3 trc, ch 4, * 3 trc in ch-lp, ch 8, sc in next lp, (ch 4, sc) in 5 ch-lps, ch 8, 3 trc over end of ch-lp, trc in trc, ch 7, sk 2 trc, trc in next trc, 3 trc in ch-lp, ch 6, sk sc, sc in next 3 sc, ch 6, 3 trc over end of ch-lp, trc in next trc, ch 7, sk 2 trc, trc in next trc. Rep from * around, end with ch 7, sl st in top of ch-4.

Rnd 80: Sl st in next 3 trc, ch 4, * 3 trc in ch-lp, ch 8, sc in next lp, (ch 4, sc) in 4 ch-lps, ch 8, 3 trc over end of ch-lp, trc in next trc, ch 6, sk 3 trc, sc in lp, ch 6, sk 3 trc, trc in next trc, 3 trc in ch-lp, ch 6, sk next sc, sc in next sc, ch 6, 3 trc over end of ch-lp, trc in next trc, ch 6, sc in ch-7 lp, ch 6, sk 3 trc, trc in next trc. Rep from * around, end as before.

Rnd 81: Sl st in next 3 trc, ch 4, 3 trc in ch-lp, * ch 8, sc in next lp, (ch 4, sc) in 3 ch-lps, ch 8, (3 trc over ch-lp, trc in trc, ch 6, sc over next lp, sc in sc, sc in next lp, ch 6, sk 3 trc, trc in next trc, 3 trc in ch-lp), ch 2; rep sts in last set of parentheses once. Rep from * around, end as before.

Rnd 82: Sl st in next 3 trc, ch 4, * 3 trc in ch-lp, ch 8, sc in next lp, (ch 4, sc) in 2 ch-lps, ch 8, 3 trc over end of ch-lp, trc in next trc, ch 6, sc over end of next lp, sc in next 3 sc, sc in lp, ch 6, sk 3 trc, trc in next trc, 2 trc in ch-2 space, trc in next trc, ch 6, sc over end of lp, sc in next 3 sc, sc in lp, ch 6, sk 3 trc, trc in next trc. Rep from * around, ending as before.

Rnd 83: Sl st in next 3 trc, ch 4, * 3 trc in ch-lp, ch 8, sc in next lp, ch 4, sc in next lp, ch 8, 3 trc over end of ch-lp, trc in next trc, (ch 7, sk 2 trc, trc in next trc, 3 trc in ch-lp, ch 6, sk sc, sc in next 3 sc, ch 6, 3 trc over end of ch-lp, trc in trc); rep sts in parentheses once; ch 7, sk 2 trc, trc in next trc. Rep from * around, end as before.

Rnd 84: Sl st in next 3 trc, ch 4, * 3 trc in ch-lp, ch 8, sc in ch-4 lp, ch 8, 3 trc over end of ch-lp, trc in trc, (ch 6, sc in lp, ch 6, sk 3 trc, trc in next trc, 3 trc in ch-lp, ch 6, sc in center sc of sc grp, ch 6, 3 trc over end of ch-lp, trc in next trc); rep sts in parentheses once; ch 6, sc in ch lp, ch 6, sk 3 trc, trc in next trc. Rep from * around, end as before.

Rnd 85: Sl st in next 3 trc, ch 4, * 3 trc in ch-lp, ch 2, 3 trc over end of next ch-lp, trc in next trc, ch 6, sc over end of lp, sc in sc, sc in next lp, ch 6, sk 3 trc, trc in next trc. Rep from * around, end as before.

Rnd 86: Sl st in 2 trc, ch 4, trc in same st as sl st, 2 trc in next trc, * 3 trc in space, 2 trc in each of next 2 trc, ch 6, sc over end of lp, sc in next 3 sc, sc in lp; (ch 8, sk 3 trc, trc in next trc, 2 trc in space, trc in trc, ch 8, sc over end of lp, sc in each of 3 sc, sc in lp), rep between parentheses once; ch 6, sk 2 trc, 2 trc in each of next 2 trc. Rep from * around, ending as before.

Rnd 87: Sl st in next 10 trc, ch 4, * 3 trc in ch-lp, ch 6, sk sc, sc in center 3 sc, ch 6, 3 trc over end of ch lp, trc in trc, [ch 7, sk 2 trc, trc in next trc, 3 trc in ch-lp, ch 6, sk sc, sc in center 3 sc, ch 6, 3 trc over end of ch-lp, trc in trc]; rep sts in [ ]s once; **(sk 1 trc, make trc, ch 2, trc in next trc—V-st made)** 4 times. Sk 1 trc, trc in next trc. Rep from * around, ending with sl st in ch-4.

Rnd 88: Sl st in next 3 trc, ch 4, * 3 trc in ch-lp, ch 6, sc in center sc of sc grp, ch 6, 3 trc over end of ch-lp, trc in next trc, (ch 6, sk 3 trc, sc in ch-7 lp, ch 6, sk 3 trc, trc in next trc, 3 trc in ch-lp, ch 6, sc in center sc, ch 6, 3 trc over end of ch-lp, trc in next trc). Rep between ( )s once, skip 3 trc; (ch 1, V-st in ch-2 sp of next V-st) 4 times; ch 1, sk 3 trc, trc in next trc. Rep from * around, ending with ch 1, sl st in top st of ch-4.

Rnd 89: Sl st in next 3 trc, ch 4, * 3 trc in ch-lp, ch 2, 3 trc over end of next ch-lp, trc in trc, (ch 8, sc over end of ch-lp, sc in sc, sc in next lp, ch 8, sk 3 trc, trc in trc, 3 trc in ch-lp, ch 2, 3 trc over end of next lp, trc in trc). Rep sts in parentheses once; ch 4, skip 3 trc (V-st in ch-2 sp of V-st, ch 4) 4 times; sk 3 trc, trc in next trc. Rep from * around, ending with ch 4, sl st in ch-4 at beg of rnd.

Rnd 90: Sl st in next 3 trc, ch 4, * 2 trc in sp, trc in next trc (ch 8, sc over end of lp, sc in next 3 sc, sc in next lp, ch 8, sk 3 trc, trc in next trc, 2 trc in sp, trc in next trc). Rep sts in parentheses once; (ch 4, V-st in ch-2 sp of V-st) 4 times; ch 4, sk 3 trc; trc in next trc. Rep from * around, end as for last rnd.

Rnd 91: Sl st in next 3 trc, ch 4, * 3 trc in ch-lp, ch 6, sk sc, sc in center 3 sc, ch 6, 3 trc over end of ch-lp, trc in trc, ch 7, sk 2 trc, trc in next trc, 3 trc in ch-lp, ch 6, sk sc, sc in center 3 sc, ch 6, 3 trc over end of ch-lp, trc in trc; (ch 6, V-st) in each of 4 V-sts, ch 6, sk 3 trc on next trc-grp, trc in next trc. Rep from * around, ending with ch 6, sl st in top of ch-4.

Rnd 92: Sl st in next 3 trc, ch 4, * 3 trc in ch-lp, ch 6, sc in center sc, ch 6, 3 trc over end of ch-lp, trc in trc, ch 6, sk sc, sc in lp, ch 6, sk 3 trc, trc

in next trc, 3 trc in ch-lp, ch 6, sk sc, sc in center sc, ch 6, 3 trc over end of ch-lp, trc in trc (ch 7, V-st) in 4 V-sts, ch 7, sk 3 trc, trc in next trc. Rep from * around; end with ch 7, sl st in top of ch-4.

Rnd 93-94: Work as for Rnds 89-90 without rep sts in parentheses and having ch 10 instead of ch 4 before and after V-sts.

Rnd 95: Sl st in 3 trc, ch 4, * 3 trc in ch-lp, ch 6, sk sc, sc in center 3 sc, ch 6, 3 trc over end of ch-lp, trc in next trc, **[ch 8 (trc, ch 2) twice, trc]** in each of 4 V-sts, ch 8, sk 3 trc, trc in next trc. Rep from * around; end as before.

Rnd 96: Sl st in next 3 trc, ch 4, * 3 trc in ch-lp, ch 6, sc in center sc, ch 6, 3 trc over end of ch-lp, trc in trc (ch 8, sk ch-8 lp, V-st in ch-2 lp, ch 2, V-st in ch-2 lp) 4 times; ch 8, sk 3 trc, trc in next trc. Rep from * around, end as before.

Rnd 97: Sl st in 3 trc, ch 4, * 3 trc in ch-lp, ch 7, trc in fifth st from hook, trc in each of next 2 ch, 3 trc over next ch-lp, trc in trc, (ch 5, sc in ch-8 lp, ch 5, V-st in V-st, ch 7, trc in fifth st from hook, trc in each of next 2 sts, V-st in next V-st) 4 times; ch 5, sc in ch-8 lp, ch 5, sk 3 trc, trc in next trc. Rep from * around, ending as before. Fasten off.

To block the finished cloth, stretch it into a circular shape and pin it to size and shape on a padded surface (such as a floor). Cover it with a damp cloth and press carefully, using a warm iron. Remove when dry.

Hexagonal-Motif Bedspread
Shown on page 34

The bedspread shown measures 72x92 inches. It is made with 200 hexagonal motifs and is sized to fit a three-quarter bed. To adjust the size, add or subtract motifs.

———— MATERIALS ————
- Coats & Clark Knit-Cro-Sheen: 14 (500-yard) balls of white
- Size 6 steel crochet hook, or size to obtain gauge

Abbreviations: See pages 26-27.
Gauge: Diameter of finished motif is 4 inches from corner to corner.

———— INSTRUCTIONS ————
Motif: With 1 strand of thread, ch 6; sl st to form ring.

Rnd 1: Ch 2, 15 dc in ring. (*Note:* Hereafter, do not join at ends of rnd.)

Rnd 2: 2 dc in top of ch-2, 2 dc in each dc around—32 dc.

Rnd 3: * Dc in first dc, 2 dc in next dc. Rep from * around—48 dc.

Rnd 4: * Ch 3, sk 1 dc, dc in next dc, 2 dc in next dc, dc in next dc; **7 dc in next dc, drop hook from work, insert hook front to back in first dc of 7-dc group and draw dropped loop through, ch 1 tightly—popcorn (pc) made.** Dc in next dc, 2 dc in next dc, dc in next dc. Rep from * around.

Rnd 5: * Ch 3, dc in first dc, 2 dc in next dc, dc in each of next 2 dc, 2 dc in the ch-1 of popcorn, dc in each of the next 2 dc, 2 dc in next dc, dc in next dc. Rep from * around.

Rnd 6: * Ch 3, dc in first dc, 2 dc in next dc, dc in next dc, popcorn in next dc, dc in each of next 4 dc, popcorn in next dc, dc in next dc, 2 dc in next dc, dc in next dc. Rep from * around.

Rnd 7: * Ch 5, dc in first dc, 2 dc in next dc, dc in each of next 10 sts, 2 dc in next dc, dc in next dc. Rep from * around, ending with sl st to beg of rnd.

Make 200 motifs. With the right sides facing, match hexagon sides and crochet motifs together into strips. Make sufficient strips for the width of the bedspread, then crochet strips together.

Tassels: Cut 18 pieces of thread, each measuring 7 inches long. Fold each thread in half; pull looped end through ch-5 sp on outer edge of bedspread, then pull cut ends through to knot tassel. Trim ends evenly.

Filet Crochet Bedspread
Shown on page 35

The finished size of the bedspread is 65x92 inches, excluding the edging. The edging is approximately 3 inches wide.

MATERIALS
- Bedspread crochet cotton: 30 (400-yard) balls of white
- Size 6 steel crochet hook, or size to obtain gauge

Abbreviations: See pages 26-27.
Gauge: 11 dc = 1 inch.

INSTRUCTIONS
Note: This bedspread is worked in strips of filet crochet. There are 12 strips, and each strip consists of 19 motif squares. The strips are sewn together when completed.

Strip: Ch 54. *Row 1:* Dc in third ch from hook, dc in each of the next 51 ch—53 dc made (turning ch counts as dc throughout); ch 2, turn.

Row 2: Sk first dc, dc in each of next 3 dc; * **ch 1, sk 1 dc, dc in next dc—space (sp) made.** Rep from * until 23 sps have been made; dc in next 2 dc and top of turning ch; ch 2, turn.

Rows 3-4: Sk first dc, dc in next 3 dc, (ch 1, dc in next dc) 23 times; dc in next 2 dc and in top of turning ch; ch 2, turn.

Row 5: Sk first dc, dc in each of next 3 dc, (ch 1, dc in next dc) 8 times; **2 hdc in ch-1 sp, dc in next dc—block (bl) over sp made;** (ch 1, dc in next dc) 5 times; 2 hdc in next ch-1 sp, dc in next dc, (ch 1, dc in next dc) 8 times; * dc in each of next 2 dc and in top of ch-2, ch 2, turn.

Note: Hereafter, work spaces and blocks in sequence specified for each row below. When making sps over bls, work in dc instead of hdc. The following guidelines contain specific instructions: **To work sp over sp,** ch 1, dc in next dc. **To work bl over sp,** work 2 hdc in ch-1 sp, dc in next dc. **To work bl over bl,** work hdc in next 2 hdc, dc in next dc. **To work sp over bl,** ch 1, sk 2 hdc, dc in next dc.

At beg of each row *always* sk the first st and beg work in second st as directed.

Row 6: Dc in each of next 3 dc, 8 sp, 2 bl, 3 sp, 2 bl, 8 sp, dc in each of next 3 dc; ch 2, turn.

Row 7: Dc in each of next 3 dc, 8 sp, 3 bl, 1 sp, 3 bl, 8 sp, dc in each of next 3 dc; ch 2, turn.

Row 8: Rep Row 7.

Row 9: Dc in each of next 3 dc, 5 sp, 3 bl, 1 sp, 2 bl, 1 sp, 2 bl, 1 sp, 3 bl, 5 sp, dc in each of next 3 dc; ch 2, turn.

Row 10: Dc in each of next 3 dc, 6 sp, 3 bl, (1 sp, 1 bl) twice; 1 sp, 3 bl, 6 sp, dc in each of next 3 dc; ch 2, turn.

Row 11: Dc in each of next 3 dc, 7 sp, 3 bl, 1 sp, 1 bl, 1 sp, 3 bl, 7 sp, dc in each of next 3 dc; ch 2, turn.

Row 12: Dc in each of next 3 dc, 10 sp, 1 bl, 1 sp, 1 bl, 10 sp, dc in each of next 3 dc; ch 2, turn.

Row 13: Rep Row 11.

Row 14: Rep Row 10.

Row 15: Rep Row 9.

Rows 16-17: Rep Row 7.

Row 18: Rep Row 6.

Row 19: Dc in each of next 3 dc; 8 sp, 1 bl, 5 sp, 1 bl, 8 sp, dc in each of next 3 dc; ch 2, turn.

Row 20: Dc in each of next 3 dc, 23 sp, dc in each of next 3 dc; ch 2, turn.

Rows 21-22: Rep Row 20.

Row 23: Dc in each of next 3 dc, * dc in next ch-1 sp, dc in next dc. Rep from * to last 3 dc, dc in each dc to end of row; ch 2, turn.

Beg with Row 2 and rep until 19 motifs are worked to complete one strip. Make 11 more strips. (Or, alter the number of strips to alter the width of the finished bedspread.)

To assemble the spread, hold strips adjacent to one another, making sure each row is aligned with its counterpart on the adjacent strip. Sew the strips together on the wrong side.

Edging: Ch 42.

Row 1: Dc in third ch from hook, and in next 37 ch—39 dc counting beg ch 2 as 1 dc. Hdc in next-to-last ch, sc in last ch; ch 2, turn.

Row 2: Sk first 2 sts; sc in first dc, ch 4, sk 1 dc, dc in next dc, (ch 1, sk 1 dc, dc in next dc) 17 times, dc in last dc and in top of turning ch; ch 3, turn.

Row 3: Sk first dc, dc in next 2 dc, (ch 1, dc in next dc) 8 times; (dc in ch-1 sp, dc in next dc) 8 times; dc in ch-1 sp, hdc in dc, sc in ch-1 sp; ch 2, turn.

Row 4: Sk first 2 sts, sc in first dc, hdc in next dc, dc in next 16 dc, (ch 1, dc in next dc) 7 times; ch 1, dc in last 2 dc and in top of turning ch; ch 3, turn.

Row 5: Sk first dc, dc in next 2 dc, (ch 1, dc in next dc) 7 times, ch 1, dc in next 14 dc, hdc in next dc, sc in last dc; ch 2, turn.

Row 6: Sk first 2 sts, sc in first dc, hdc in next dc, dc in next 12 dc, (ch 1, dc in next dc) 7 times; ch 1, dc in last 3 dc; ch 3, turn.

Row 7: Sk first dc, dc in next 2 dc, (ch 1, dc in next dc) 7 times; ch 1, dc in next 10 dc, hdc in next dc, sc in last dc; ch 2, turn.

Row 8: Sk first 2 sts, sc in first dc, hdc in next dc, dc in next 8 dc, (ch 1, dc in next dc) 7 times; ch 1, dc in last 3 dc; ch 3, turn.

Row 9: Sk first dc, dc in next 2 dc, (ch 1, dc in next dc) 7 times; ch 1, dc in next 6 dc, hdc in next dc, sc in last dc; ch 2, turn.

Row 10: Sk first 2 sts, sc in first dc, hdc in next dc, dc in next 4 dc; (dc in ch-1 sp, dc in next dc) 7 times; ch 1, dc in last 3 dc; ch 3, turn.

Row 11: Sk first dc, dc in next 2 dc, ch 1, (dc in next dc) 16 times; hdc in next dc, sc in last dc; ch 2, turn.

Row 12: Sk first 2 sts, sc in first dc, hdc in next dc, (dc in next dc) 14 times; ch 1, dc in last 3 dc; ch 3, turn.

Row 13: Sk first dc, dc in next 2 dc, ch 1, (dc in next dc) 12 times; hdc in next dc, sc in last dc; ch 2, turn.

Row 14: Sk the first 2 sts, sc in first dc, hdc in next dc, (dc in next dc) 10 times; ch-1, dc in the last 3 dc; ch 3, turn.

Row 15: Sk first dc, dc in next 2 dc, ch 1, (dc in next dc) 8 times; hdc in next dc, sc in last dc; ch 2, turn.

Row 16: Sk first 2 sts, sc in first dc, hdc in next dc, (dc in next dc) 6 times; ch 1, dc in last 3 dc. At this point, to extend length of edging, ch 33; turn.

Row 17 (extension): Dc in third ch from hook, and in each ch across; dc in next 3 dc—35 dc made; ch 1, dc in next 4 dc, hdc in next dc, sc in last dc; ch 2, turn.

Row 18: Sk first 2 sts, sc in first dc, hdc in next dc, (dc in next dc) 2 times; ch 1, dc in next dc, (ch 1, sk dc, dc in next dc) 15 times; ch 1, sk dc, dc in next 2 dc and in top of turning ch; ch 3, turn.

Row 19: Sk first dc, dc in next 2 dc, (ch 1, dc in next dc) 7 times; ch 1, (dc in next dc, dc in ch-1 sp) 9 times; hdc in dc, sc in last dc; ch 2, turn.

Row 20: Sk first 2 sts, sc in first dc, hdc in next dc (dc in next dc) 16 times; (ch 1, dc in next dc) 7 times; ch 1, dc in last 3 dc; ch 3, turn.

Row 21: Sk first dc, dc in next 2 dc, (ch 1, dc in next dc) 7 times; ch 1

(dc in next dc) 14 times; hdc in dc, sc in last dc; ch 2, turn.

Row 22: Sk first 2 sts, sc in first dc, hdc in next dc, (dc in next dc) 12 times; (ch 1, dc in next dc) 7 times; ch 1, dc in last 3 dc; ch 3, turn.

Row 23: Sk first dc, dc in next 2 dc, (ch 1, dc in next dc) 7 times; ch 1, (dc in next dc) 10 times; hdc in dc, sc in last dc; ch 2, turn.

Row 24: Sk first 2 sts, sc in first dc, hdc in next dc, (dc in next dc) 8 times; (ch 1, dc in next dc) 7 times; ch 1, dc in last 3 dc; ch 3, turn.

Row 25: Sk first dc, dc in next 2 dc, (ch 1, dc in next dc) 7 times; ch 1, (dc in next dc) 6 times; hdc in dc; sc in last dc; ch 2, turn.

Rows 26-31: Rep Rows 10-15.

Rep Rows 16-31 to extend edging to desired length. Work 4 separate strips. (Bedspread shown features edging around all 4 sides.)

When the length of the edging equals that of the motif strip, complete the pattern through Row 15, then complete the last triangles as follows:

Row 16: Sk first 2 sts, sc in next dc, hdc in next dc, (dc in next dc) 6 times; ch 1, dc in last 3 dc; ch 3, turn.

Row 17: Sk first dc, dc in next 2

dc, ch 1 (dc in next dc) 4 times, hdc in next dc, sc in last dc; ch 2, turn.

Row 18: Sk first 2 sts, sc in next dc, hdc in next dc, (dc in next dc) twice; ch 1, dc in last 3 dc. Fasten off.

Finishing: With the right side of the edging strip facing you, attach crochet thread at the righthand edge.

Row 1: Sc in each st along the straight edge of the edging and work approximately 46 sc on each section of Rows 1-18 (base of each triangle section); ch 4, turn.

Row 2: Sk first sc, dc in next sc, * ch 1, sk 1 sc, dc in next sc. Rep from * across; ch 3, turn.

Row 3: Dc in first ch-1 sp, dc in dc, * dc in ch-1 sp, dc in dc. Rep from * across, ending with dc in turning ch-4 sp, dc in third ch of ch-4; ch 4, turn.

Row 4: Sk first 2 dc, dc in next dc, ch 1, * sk dc, dc in next dc, ch 1. Rep from * across, ending with dc in top of turning ch-3; ch 1, turn.

Row 5: * Sc in ch-1 sp, sc in next dc. Rep from * across, ending with sc in turning ch-4 sp, sc in third of ch-4. Fasten off.

With right sides facing up, sew edging to assembled strips.

◆ How to Care for Handmade Lace ◆

To preserve the beauty of the crocheted lace you've made yourself, treat it with the same tender, loving care that you would lavish on the heirloom laces in your linen cupboard.

Repair all damaged lace before washing it. If sewing is adequate to repair the damage, insert the needle *between* threads rather than into them.

Holes are best repaired by darning: Using a thread close to the color and weight of the original, weave horizontal threads across the tear; begin and end

with three or more meshes on each side of the hole. Weave in and out of these threads, duplicating the original stitches as closely as possible.

To remove stains, use a gentle bleach, such as lemon juice mixed with water. Or, use hydrogen peroxide, diluting it according to the manufacturer's directions.

You also can remove stains using a weak solution of non-chlorine household bleach. Begin with one teaspoon of bleach per cup of water. Soak the lace only long enough to remove the stain.

Home dry cleaning will remove some stains that won't disappear in water solutions. Before applying a dry-cleaning product, read the label directions carefully.

Store your handmade lace in a cool, dry place. Lay small pieces flat, without folding, between sheets of acid-free tissue paper. Loosely roll larger pieces around a cardboard or wooden cylinder that has been wrapped with tissue paper. Wrap another layer of tissue paper around the outside of the lace.

WARM, COZY SWEATERS

for all the family

During summer's cool breezes or
winter's chilling frosts, every member of your
family will snuggle comfortably in the
crocheted fashions shown here.
Delightful patterns and soft textures set
off each of these classic, easy-to-make designs.
Besides cover-ups for toddlers,
and a coordinating sweater set for the family,
there are his-and-hers styles, like
matching pullovers, *left*.

Subtle stripes in neutral shades are worked
in single crochet. For an added accent,
stripes on the lower body portion are worked
through the back loops to create
textured ridges along the rows. For wearable
styling, the sweaters feature dropped
shoulders and ribbings at the
waistline, neckband, and cuffs.
Instructions for sweaters begin on page 54.

◆ ◆ ◆

For those brisk around-the-block walks or journeys to the playground you will want a cozy wrap to keep your children warm. The hooded jackets and pullovers shown here look just like the ones grown-ups wear, with sophisticated striping and coloring, but they come in toddler sizes only.

The budding ballerinas, *above,* warm up at the bar dressed in matching, multistriped pullovers. To create the striped effect, work rows of single crochet and chain stitches on the diagonal, changing colors as you go.

The his-and-hers jackets, *opposite,* are sure-fire staples in any kid's wardrobe. Zippered fronts make them easy to slip on and off, and the drawstring hoods snug up close on cold or windy days. Work the body in one piece, the yoke and sleeves in another; then sew the sections together.

◆ ◆ ◆

For looks that keep their polish even on the busiest days, nothing beats the free, easygoing style of crisp, cotton pullovers. Bright, clear colors give this spirited set of family sweaters lots of impact, and add zest to any number of separates, from everyday blue jeans and khakis to sporty skirts and dressy casuals.

Though these sprightly stripes and checkerboard patterns appear to be complicated, they are easily worked in half-double crochet stitches with single crocheted ribbing accents.

To create the adult-size pullovers, crochet the checkerboard pattern in vertical strips and whipstitch the strips together. For the child's version, stitch back and forth with bobbins, changing colors as you crochet.

Such a snappy design is too special to save for summer only. With a few changes, you can crochet it for any season. For example, substitute heather-tone yarns for the colors shown here for sweaters that slip into fall. Or, dip into your remnant bag for cotton or sport-weight yarns left over from other projects. Use these scraps for the pullovers, varying the checkerboard colors and changing the colors of the stripes from row to row to create sweaters with a look that's different.

Instructions for all the pullovers include small, medium, and large sizes.

WARM, COZY SWEATERS

When the first chill of autumn arrives, your family can step out in style in one of these richly textured cover-ups. Crocheted in classic, easy-to-wear neutrals, these fashions mix and match beautifully with just about everything in a fall wardrobe.

Earth tones such as taupe, brown, gray, and charcoal accentuate the textures and patterns in these designs and highlight the natural shaping of each garment.

Work the versatile spencer jacket, *opposite,* in single crochet stitches, using nubby yarn for the look and feel of real lamb's wool. Slightly padded shoulders and a cropped-in waist make it a smart fashion accessory.

The man's V-neck cardigan, *above,* is worked in an overall pattern of chain and single crochet stitches. Long, lean styling makes this sweater especially comfortable to wear.

Worked in double crochet and popcorn stitches, the sporty cardigan, *right,* is tapered at the waist for a gently flattering fit.

His-and-Hers Pullovers
Shown on pages 46-47

Directions are for woman's size Small (6-8); changes for women's sizes Medium (10-12) and Large (14-16), and men's sizes Small (36-38), Medium (40-42), and Large (44-46) follow in parentheses. Bust = 31½ (34, 38) inches; chest = 38 (42, 46) inches.

MATERIALS
· Reynolds Lopi Light (50-gram balls), or a suitable substitute: 11 (12, 13, 13, 14, 15) balls of No. 409 beige (MC), 1 ball each of Nos. 403 taupe (A) and 408 light brown (B)
· Size H aluminum crochet hook, or size to obtain gauge

Abbreviations: See pages 26-27.
Gauge: 7 sc = 2 inches; 4 rows = 1 inch.

INSTRUCTIONS
• These sweaters feature dropped shoulders, so there is no armhole shaping.

Back—*Ribbing:* With MC, ch 13.

Row 1: Sc in second ch from hook and in each ch across—12 sts; ch 1, turn. *Row 2:* Working in back lps only, sc in each st across; ch 1, turn. Rep Row 2 until 60 (66, 74, 70, 76, 84) rows are completed. Do not fasten off. Working along long edge of ribbing strip, sc in end of each row across—60 (66, 74, 70, 76, 84) sts.

Working in back lps throughout, work 3 more rows in MC, * 2 rows A, 4 rows MC, 2 rows B, 4 rows MC. Rep from * 4 times more, or until desired length to underarm, ending on wrong side. Mark last row. Work even in MC, working through both lps until piece measures 7½ (7½, 8, 9, 10, 11) inches above marker, ending on wrong side.

Shoulder shaping: * Sl st across first 10 (11, 12, 8, 9, 10) sts; work in sc across row to within last 10 (11, 12, 8, 9, 10) sts. Do not ch; turn. Rep from * once more. *For men's sizes only:* Sl st across first (7, 8, 9) sts, work in sc across row to within last (7, 8, 9) sts. Fasten off.

Front: Work same as for back until total length past marker measures 4 (4, 4½, 6, 7, 8) inches.

Neck shaping: Work to center 10 (10, 10, 12, 12, 12) sts; sk center 10 (10, 10, 12, 12, 12) sts, join a second ball of yarn, work across rem sts. Working both sides separately, dec 1 st at each neck edge every other row 5 (6, 8, 6, 6, 7) times. Work even until total length past marker equals that of back. Shape shoulders as for back. Fasten off.

Sleeves: With MC, work in ribbing as for back for 24 (24, 26, 30, 33, 36) rows. Working along long edge of ribbing, work 1 sc in end of each row—24 (24, 26, 30, 33, 36) sts. *Next row:* Work 2 sc in each sc across—48 (48, 52, 60, 66, 72) sts.

Following 2 rows: Inc 1 st at each edge of next 2 rows—52 (52, 56, 64, 70, 76) sts. Working even, * work 6 rows of sc through back lps, 4 rows of sc through both lps, 4 rows of sc through back lps, 4 rows of sc through both lps. Rep from * until total length measures 16 (17, 18, 17½, 18½, 19) inches, or desired length to underarm.

Finishing: Sew shoulder seams.

Neck ribbing: With MC, ch 5. Working over 4 sc, work as for ribbing of back until piece, when slightly stretched, reaches around neck edge, ending with an uneven number of rows; fasten off, leaving a 6-inch tail. Sew ends of ribbing together. Pin to neckline and sew in place. Sew sleeve tops to sweater, easing width of sleeve tops between markers, if necessary. Sew side and sleeve seams.

Child's Pullover
Shown on page 48

Directions are for size Small (2); changes for sizes Medium (4) and Large (6) follow in parentheses. Chest = 21 (23, 24½) inches.

MATERIALS
· Bucilla Winsom (2-ounce balls), or a suitable substitute: 2 (2, 3) balls of color A; 1 ball each of colors B and C for all sizes
· Size G aluminum crochet hook, or size to obtain gauge

Abbreviations: See pages 26-27.
Gauge: 5 sts = 1 inch; 4 rows = 1 inch.

INSTRUCTIONS
Body (make 2 pieces): With B, ch 2. *Row 1* (right side): Work sc, ch 1, sc in second ch from hook; ch 1, turn. *Row 2:* In first sc work sc, ch 1, sc; sk ch-1 sp, work sc, ch 1, sc in last st—4 sts. Drop B; join C.

Row 3: With C, ch 1, turn; sc in first st, * ch 1, sc in next sc; rep from * across; ch 1, turn.

Row 4: Work **sc, ch 1, sc all in first st—inc made;** * ch 1, sc in next sc; rep from * across, ending with ch 1, sc, ch 1, sc all in last st—6 sts. Drop C; join A, ch 1, turn.

Row 5: Work even. Continuing to work in stripe pat of 2 rows C, 2 rows B, and 1 row A, rep Rows 4 and 3 (increasing every other row) until there are 26 (28, 32) rows from beg—28 (30, 34) sts. Place a marker for 1 corner.

Note: To work a dec, draw up a lp in each of the next 2 sts, yo, draw through 3 lps on hook.

Rows 27-33 (29-35, 33-39): Working in pat as established, dec 1 st at beg of row and inc 1 st at end of row—7 decs and 7 incs made. Work 1 row even.

Next row: Dec 1 st each side. Rep last row until 1 sc, ch 1, 1 sc rem. *Final row:* Draw up a lp in each sc, yo, and draw through all 3 lps on hook. Fasten off.

Back yoke: With A, from right side, join yarn at upper right corner of back, work across in pat having 51 (55, 61) sc across and 50 (54, 60) ch-1 sps, to include sc at end of row. Ch 1, turn. Work even for 8 (9, 10) rows. *Neck shaping:* Work across 15 (17, 19) sts; ch 1, turn. Working on these 15 (17, 19) sts only, work even for 6 (7, 7) rows; fasten off. Sk center 21 (21, 23) sts for neck, join A, and work other side to correspond.

Front yoke: Work same as for back.

Sleeves: With A, ch 46 (48, 50). *Row 1:* Work sc in second ch from hook, * ch 1, sk 1 ch, sc in next ch; rep from * across; ch 1, turn.

Row 2: Work sc in first sc, * ch 1, sc in next sc. Rep from * across, ending with 1 sc. Ch 1, turn. Rep

Row 2 for pat. Work even until total length from beg measures 11 (12, 13) inches, or desired length to underarm. Fasten off.

Finishing: Sew shoulder seams. Sew in sleeves, marking off 4½ (4¾, 5) inches from shoulder on each side for armhole depth. Sew side and sleeve seams.

Edging: Beg at center back of neck, work 1 row of reverse sc (work from left to right) around entire neck edge, dec 1 st in each corner st. Fasten off. From wrong side of sleeve edge, work 1 row of reverse sc around lower edge. Turn up cuffs.

Child's Jacket
Shown on page 49

Directions are for size Small (2); changes for sizes Medium (4) and Large (6) follow in parentheses. Chest = 22 (25, 26) inches.

————— **MATERIALS** —————
- Bucilla Horizon (2-ounce balls): 2 (2, 2) balls of color A
- Bucilla Twin-Pak Win Knit (4-ounce package: 1 (1, 2) packages of color B; 1 package each of colors C and D for all sizes
- Size G aluminum crochet hook, or size to obtain gauge
- Separating zipper

Abbreviations: See pages 26-27.
Gauge: 4 sts = 1 inch; 5 rows = 1 inch.

————— **INSTRUCTIONS** —————
Note: Jacket body is worked in one piece, beginning at right front edge around to left front edge. Yoke and sleeves are worked across from sleeve edge to sleeve edge.
Body: With D, ch 36 (40, 44).
Row 1: Sc in second ch from hook and in each rem ch across; ch 1, turn—35 (39, 43) sts.
Row 2: Sc in each sc across; ch 1, turn. Rep Row 2 for pat. Including first 2 rows of D at beg, work in the fol color sequence: * 3 (4, 4) rows D; 5 (5, 6) rows A; 1 row C; 4 rows B; 5 rows D; 5 (6, 6) rows A; 1 row C; and 3 rows B *. Mark last row as right underarm. Rep bet *s once, revers-

ing color stripes by beg rep with 3 rows B and ending with 3 (4, 4) rows D. Mark last row for center back. Rep bet *s once, beg with 3 (4, 4) rows D and ending with 3 rows B. Mark last row as left underarm. Rep bet *s, reversing color stripes as before, beg with 3 rows B and ending with 3 (4, 4) rows D—108 (116, 120) rows from beg. Fasten off.
Back yoke and sleeves: With B, ch 126 (137, 149). Work in sc in the fol color sequence: 3 (3, 4) rows B; 2 rows D; 2 rows C; 2 rows D; 4 (5, 5) rows A; 2 rows C; 2 rows A; 2 (3, 3) rows C; and 5 (6, 6) rows B—24 (27, 28) rows. Mark off center 45 (49, 53) sts for back of neck. Rem sts on each side are for sleeves and shoulders. Fasten off.
Right front yoke and sleeve: Ch 64 (69, 74). Work in color stripe sequence as for back yoke until third C stripe is completed, ending at center edge—63 (68, 73) sts. *Neck shaping:* At center edge, sl st across 2, (3, 3) sts. Dec 1 st at same edge every row 3 (4, 4) times as follows: **Draw up lp in each of next 2 sc, yo, draw through 3 lps on hook —dec made.** Work even until total length equals that of back yoke and sleeve. Fasten off.
Left front yoke and sleeve: Work to correspond to right front yoke and sleeve, reversing shaping.
Hood: With D, ch 39 (45, 51). Work in sc pat in the fol color stripe sequence: 4 (4, 5) rows D; 4 rows C; 2 rows B; 1 row C; 2 rows A; 4 (4, 5) rows B; 2 rows A; 4 (5, 6) rows C; 4 rows D; 2 rows B; 1 row C; 4 rows B; 4 (5, 5) rows C; 2 rows B; 2 rows C; and 3 rows D—45 (47, 50) rows. Fasten off, leaving a 10-inch length for sewing across top hood seam. Sew seam.
Edging: From right side, with D, work 1 sc in each row across front of hood. Work sc for 7 rows. Work 1 row C, then 2 rows B. Fasten off.
Finishing: Sew top yoke seams. Sew underarms 10 (12, 13) inches from cuff. Sew lower edge of yoke to top of body, matching underarm seams to markers. From right side with B, and beg at left back edge, work 1 row sc along left front, * 3 sc

in corner *, sc along bottom edge. Rep bet *s, sc along right front edge. Fasten off. Sew hood 1 inch in from front neck edges, easing to fit. Steam lightly.

At cuff edge from wrong side, with B, work 3 rnds sc. Fasten off. Turn back cuffs, sew zipper in place to front edges.
Drawstring: With 2 strands of B, make a 40-inch ch. Fasten off. Weave through second row of B at front edge of hood.
Tassel: Wind A, B, and C around a 5-inch cardboard square approximately 20 times. Using 2 strands of B, tie at 1 end; cut opposite end. Wind tassel with B ¾ inch from tied end. With 2 strands of B, make a 3-inch ch, attach to tassel. Sew to point of hood.

His-and-Hers Checkerboard Pullovers
Shown on page 50

In the directions that follow, the instructions for both the men's and women's sizes are the same. However, the hook size for each varies, which results in the differences in the finished sizes of the sweaters. Directions are for woman's size Small (8-10) and man's size Small (36); changes for sizes Medium for women (12-14) and men (38-40) and Large for women (16) and men (42-44) follow in the parentheses. Bust sizes for women = 31½-32½, (34-36), (38) inches. Chest sizes for men = 36, (38-40), (42-44) inches.

————— **MATERIALS** —————
- *For women:* Coats and Clark Red Heart 100% cotton knit and crochet yarn, or a suitable substitute: 15 (16, 17) ounces No. 001 white; 10 (10, 11) ounces No. 662 kelly green; 5 (5, 6) ounces No. 910 red
- *For men:* Coats and Clark Red Heart 100% cotton knit and crochet yarn, or a suitable substitute: 17½ (20, 22) ounces No. 662 kelly green; 20 (22½, 25) ounces No. 001 white

continued

- *For women:* Size E aluminum crochet hook, or size to obtain gauge
- *For men:* Size G aluminum crochet hook, or size to obtain gauge
- Package of yarn bobbins

Abbreviations: See pages 26-27.
Gauge: *Size E hook:* 9 hdc = 2 inches; 13 hdc rows = 4 inches.
Size G hook: 4 hdc = 1 inch; 3 hdc rows = 1 inch.

INSTRUCTIONS

The checkerboard pattern on the lower sections of the back, front, and sleeve pieces is made in strips, then the strips are sewn together. The stripe pattern on the upper section is worked across the top edge of each completed checkerboard piece. The ribbings are made separately and sewn to the lower edges.

Back (lower section), Strip A—make 6 (6, 7): Beg at lower edge with green, ch 8.

Foundation row: Sc in second ch from hook and in each ch across—7 sc; ch 2, turn. *Row 1* (right side): Hdc in each st across—7 hdc; do not count ch-2 as a st. *Rows 2-3:* Rep Row 1.

Row 4: Hdc in each hdc across to last hdc; **yo, draw up a lp in last hdc, drop green; with white, yo, draw through the rem 3 lps on hook—color change made;** with white, ch 2, turn.

Rows 5-8: Rep Rows 1-4, changing to green in last hdc of last row; with green, ch 2, turn. Rep last 8 rows 3 times more, then Rows 1-4 once more. Fasten off.

Strip B—make 5 (6, 6): Beg with white, work as for Strip A until Row 4 is completed. Change to green at end of Row 4; with green, ch 2, turn.

Rows 5-8: Rep Rows 1-4 of Strip A; with white, ch 2, turn. Complete as for Strip A.

Joining strips: Beg at lower edge with right sides facing, sew long edges of Strip A and Strip B together. Alternating strips, continue to join rem strips in this manner to form checkerboard pat.

Upper stripe and raglan armhole shaping—*Row 1:* With right side of lower section facing, sk first 2 (2, 3) hdc at top edge. Join red to next st for woman's sweater, (join green for man's sweater), ch 2, hdc in joining. Keeping work flat, make 73 (80, 85) hdc across to last 2 (2, 3) hdc; do not work over these sts—74 (81, 86) hdc; ch 1, turn.

Row 2: **Draw up a lp in first hdc, yo, draw up a lp in next hdc, yo, and draw through all 4 lps on hook—dec made at beg of row;** hdc in each hdc to last 2 hdc; **draw up a lp in next hdc, yo, draw up a lp in last hdc, drop color in use; with white, draw through all lps on hook—dec and color change made.** (Carry color not in use loosely along side edge.) With white, ch 1, turn.

Row 3: Dec 1 hdc at beg of row, hdc in each hdc across to last 2 hdc on row; **draw up a lp in next hdc, yo, draw up a lp in last hdc, yo, and draw through all rem lps on hook—dec made at end of row;** ch 1, turn.

Row 4: Work as for Row 2 of raglan shaping, changing to red at end of row for woman's sweater, (change to green for man's sweater); with new color, ch 2, turn.

Row 5: Work as for Row 3; ch 1, turn. Rep Rows 2-5 of pat 5 (6, 6) times more. Work 0 (0, 1) row even. Fasten off.

Front, lower section: Work 6 (6, 7) strips as for Strip B and 5 (6, 6) strips as for Strip A of back.

Beg with Strip B, and alternating strips, join strips as for back.

Upper stripe and raglan armhole shaping: Work as for raglan armhole shaping of back until 14 (18, 20) rows of armhole shaping are worked—46 (45, 46) hdc; ch 2, turn.

First neck shaping: *Row 1:* Working in stripe pat, dec at raglan edge, hdc in next 16 (15, 16) hdc; do not work over rem sts; ch 2, turn. Dec 1 hdc at each end of next row and every row until 5 (6, 3) hdc rem. Keeping neck edge straight, continue to dec at raglan edge until 2 sts rem; ch 2, turn. *Last row:* Dec over last 2 sts. Fasten off.

Second neck shaping: With right side facing, sk the center 11 (12, 11) hdc on last long row

worked, join corresponding color yarn to next st, ch 2, hdc in same place where yarn was joined; hdc in each hdc across, dec 1 hdc at raglan edge; ch 1, turn. Complete to correspond to other side.

Sleeves (lower section), first strip—make 1: Beg at lower edge with green, ch 8, (10, 5).

Foundation row (right side): Sc in second ch from hook and in each ch across—7 (9, 4) sc; ch 2, turn.

Rows 1-8: Working over 7 (9, 4) sts, work as for Rows 1-8 of Strip A of back until 48 (52, 52) rows above foundation row are completed. Fasten off.

Strip B—make 3 (3, 4): Work as for Strip B of back until 48 (52, 52) rows above foundation row are completed.

Strip A—make 3 (3, 4): Beg with white, work as for previous strip.

Last strip: Beg with white, work as for first strip of sleeve. There are 8 (8, 10) strips. With right sides facing, beg at lower edge and join strips as for back, having first and last strip at each end.

Upper stripe and raglan top shaping—*Row 1:* With right side facing, sk first 2 (2, 3) hdc at top edge of lower section, join red to next st for woman's sweater (green for man's sweater), ch 2, hdc in joining, keeping work flat, make 52 (56, 58) hdc across to last 2 (2, 3) hdc, do not work over these sts; ch 1, turn. Rep Rows 2-5 of back raglan armhole shaping 4 times. Continuing in stripe pat, dec 1 hdc at each end on next row and every other row 5 (6, 7) times in all. Fasten off.

Pin separate pieces to measurements, dampen, and leave to dry. Matching patterns, sew side, sleeve, and raglan seams.

Lower ribbing: Beg at lower edge with white, ch 14 (16, 16). *Row 1:* Sc in second st from hook and in each ch across—13 (15, 15) sc; ch 1, turn. *Row 2:* Sc in back lp of each sc across; ch 1, turn. Rep Row 2 until ribbing when slightly stretched is 28 (31, 33) inches for woman's sweater (37, 41, 45 inches for man's sweater). Fasten off. Sew narrow edges of ribbing with a side seam, sew 1 edge of ribbing to lower edge of pullover, easing in top to fit.

Sleeve ribbing—make 2: Work as for lower ribbing until piece measures 6½ (7, 7½) inches for woman's sweater (8, 8, 8½ inches for man's sweater). Fasten off. Sew narrow edges together. Sew to lower edge of sleeves, easing sleeves to fit.

Neck ribbing: Beg at narrow edge with red (green for man's sweater), ch 9. Working over 8 sc, work as for lower ribbing until total length is 19½ (19½, 20) inches for woman's sweater (19, 20, 21 inches for man's sweater). Fasten off. Sew narrow edges tog. Sew 1 long edge to neck edge.

Child's Checkerboard Pullover

Shown on page 51

Directions are for Size 4; changes for Sizes 6, 8, and 10 follow in parentheses. Chest size = 23 (24, 26, 28) inches.

———————MATERIALS———————
- Coats & Clark Red Heart 100% cotton knit and crochet yarn, or a suitable substitute: 8 (9, 10, 12) ounces of No. 001 white, and 2½ (3, 4, 5) ounces each of Nos. 910 red and 662 kelly green
- Size F aluminum crochet hook, or size to obtain gauge
- Package of yarn bobbins

Abbreviations: See pages 26-27.
Gauge: 4 hdc = 1 inch; 3 rows = 1 inch.

——————INSTRUCTIONS——————
Back—*Ribbing:* Beg at narrow edge with white, ch 13 (16, 16, 16), having 5 sts per inch.
Row 1: Sc in second ch from hook and in each ch across—12 (15, 15, 15) sc; ch 1, turn. *Row 2:* Sc in *back* lp of each sc across; ch 1, turn.
Rep Row 2 until total length is 11½ (12, 13, 14) inches. At end of last row, do not turn.
Foundation row: Ch 1, make 50 (52, 56, 60) sc evenly spaced across next long edge of ribbing; ch 2,

turn. Wind 4 bobbins each with red, white, and green and work checkerboard pat as follows:
Back—*Row 1* (wrong side): Hdc in first 4 (5, 7, 9) sts; **yo, draw up a lp in next st, drop white to wrong side of work; with red, yo and draw through rem 3 lps on hook—color change made;** * with red, hdc in next 8 sts, changing to white in last hdc; with white, hdc in next 8 sts, changing to red in last hdc. Rep from * across, ending last rep with white and hdc in last 5 (6, 8, 10) sc—50 (52, 56, 60) hdc, not counting ch-2 as a st; ch 2, turn.
Row 2: With white, hdc in first 5 (6, 8, 10) hdc, changing to red in last hdc; * with red, hdc in next 8 hdc, changing to white in last hdc; with white, hdc in next 8 hdc, changing to red in last hdc. Rep from * across, ending with white, hdc in last 5 (6, 8, 10) hdc; with white, ch 2, turn.
Row 3: Rep Row 1.
Row 4: Rep Row 2, changing to green in last hdc; with green, ch 2, turn. Cut all red strands and weave in on wrong side of work.
Row 5: With green, hdc in first 5 (6, 8, 10) hdc, changing to white in last hdc; * with white, hdc in next 8 hdc, changing to green in last hdc; with green, hdc in the next 8 hdc, changing to white in last hdc. Rep from * across, ending with green, hdc in last 5 (6, 8, 10) hdc; with green, ch 2, turn.
Rows 6-7: Rep Row 5. *Row 8:* Rep Row 5, changing to white in last hdc; with white, ch 2, turn. Rep last 8 rows 1 (1, 2, 2) times more. *For Sizes 8 and 10 only:* Rep Rows 1-4, once more changing to white in last hdc. Cut all red or green strands and weave into back of work. *For all sizes:* With white, ch 1, turn.
Stripe pattern and raglan armhole shaping—*Row 1:* Sl st across first 2 sts, ch 2, hdc in next 46 (48, 52, 56) sts, changing to green in last hdc; do not work over rem 2 hdc; with green, ch 2, turn.
Row 2: **Draw up a lp in first hdc, yo, draw up a lp in next hdc, yo, and draw through all 4 lps on hook—dec made at beg of row;** hdc in each hdc across to last 2 hdc; **draw up a lp in next hdc, yo, draw up a lp in last hdc, drop**

green; with white, yo and draw through all 4 lps on hook—dec and color change made at end of row; with white, ch 2, turn.
Row 3: With white, rep Row 2, changing to red in last hdc; with red, ch 2, turn. *Row 4:* With red, rep Row 2, changing to white in last hdc; with white, ch 2, turn.
Row 5: Rep Row 2, changing to green in last hdc; ch 2, turn. Rep last 4 rows for stripe pat throughout. Continuing in stripe pat, dec 1 hdc at each end of every row 5 (7, 9, 11) times more—28 (26, 26, 26) hdc.
First neck shaping—*Row 1:* Dec 1 hdc at raglan edge; hdc in next 4 hdc; do not work over rem sts; ch 1, turn. *Row 2:* Dec 1 hdc at each end, work across; ch 1, turn. *Row 3:* Dec 1 hdc at raglan edge. Fasten off.
Second neck shaping—*Row 1:* Sk center 16 (14, 14, 14) hdc on last long row worked; join corresponding color yarn to next st; ch 2, hdc in same place as join; hdc in each hdc across, dec 1 hdc at raglan edge; turn. Complete to correspond to other side.
Front: Work same as for back until foundation row is completed; with red, ch 2, turn.
Rows 1-4: Using red instead of white and white instead of red, work as for Rows 1-4 of back, changing to white in last hdc of last row; with white, ch 2, turn. *Rows 5-8:* Using white instead of green and green instead of white, work as for Rows 5-8 of back. Work as for back to raglan armhole shaping.
Stripe pattern and raglan armhole shaping—*Rows 1-5:* Rep Rows 1-5 of back raglan armhole shaping. Continuing in stripe pat, dec 1 hdc at each end of every row 3 (5, 7, 9) times more.
First neck shaping—*Row 1:* Dec 1 hdc at armhole edge, hdc in next 9 hdc; do not work over rem sts; turn. *Row 2:* Sl st across first 2 sts, ch 2, hdc in each st across, dec 1 hdc at raglan edge; ch 1, turn.
Row 3: Dec 1 hdc at each end, work across; ch 1, turn. *Row 4:* Rep Row 3. *Row 5:* Dec 1 hdc at raglan edge. Fasten off.

continued

Second neck shaping—*Row 1:* Sk the center 10 (8, 8, 8) sts on last long row worked, join corresponding color yarn to next st, ch 2, hdc in same place as join; hdc in each hdc across, dec 1 hdc at raglan edge; ch 2, turn. *Row 2:* Dec at raglan edge; hdc across to last 2 hdc; do not work these sts; ch 2, turn. Complete as for opposite side.

Sleeves—*Ribbing:* Beg at side edge, with white, ch 9 (9, 11, 13). Working over 8 (8, 10, 12) sc, work as for ribbing on back until piece measures 5 (5, 5½, 5½) inches; at end of last row do *not* turn.

Foundation row: Ch 1, sc 34 (36, 38, 40) sts evenly spaced across next long edge of ribbing; ch 2, turn.

Row 1: With white, hdc in first 5 (6, 7, 8) sts, changing to green in last st; * with green, hdc in next 8 st, changing to white in last hdc; with white, hdc in next 8 sts, changing to green in last hdc. Rep from * across, ending with white, hdc in last 5 (6, 7, 8) sts; with white, ch 2, turn.

Rows 2-4: Rep Row 1. At end of last row, change to red in last hdc. With red, ch 2, turn.

Row 5: **2 hdc in first hdc—inc made;** hdc in next 4 (5, 6, 7) hdc, change to white in last hdc; * with white, hdc in next 8 hdc, change to red in last hdc; with red, hdc in next 8 hdc, change to white in last hdc. Rep from * across, end with red, hdc in next 4 (5, 6, 7) hdc, inc in last hdc; with red, ch 2, turn. *Rows 6-8:* Work even in established colors. At end of last row, change to red in last hdc; with red, ch 2, turn.

Rep last 8 rows for checkerboard pat; *at same time* inc 1 hdc at each end on next row and every sixth row once more—40 (42, 44, 46) hdc. Continue in pat, working 28 (28, 32, 36) rows above foundation row.

Stripe pattern and raglan top shaping: Work as for raglan top shaping for back until 12 (10, 16, 18) sts rem. *For Sizes 8 and 10 only:* Continue in pat and dec 1 hdc at each end of every other row until 12 hdc rem. *For all sizes:* Fasten off.

Pin all the pieces to measurements, dampen, and leave to dry. Matching patterns, sew side and sleeve seams. Sew raglan seams.

Neckband: With white, ch 7. Work 6 sc for ribbing as on back until piece measures 18 (18, 19, 19) inches. Fasten off. Sew the narrow edges of band tog. Sew 1 long edge of neckband to neck edge.

Spencer Jacket
Shown on page 52

Directions are for size Small (6-8). Changes for sizes Medium (10-12) and Large (14-16) are in parentheses. Bust measurements = 30½-31½ (32½-34, 36-38) inches.

MATERIALS
- Coats & Clark Red Heart Bulky Loop Yarn, or a suitable substitute (3-ply, 50-gram balls): 12 (14, 15) balls of No. 33 oxford
- Size J crochet hook
- 1 button, 1 inch in diameter
- 2 shoulder pads (optional)

Abbreviations: See pages 26-27.
Gauge: 5 sc = 2 inches; 3 rows = 1 inch.

INSTRUCTIONS
Back: Beg at lower edge, ch 37 (41, 45) to measure 15 (16½, 18) inches. *Row 1:* Sc in second ch from hook and in each ch across—36 (40, 44) sc. Mark row for right side. Ch 1, turn. *Rows 2-3:* Sc in each sc. Ch 1, turn. *Row 4:* **Draw up a loop in each of first 2 sc, yo, and draw through 3 loops on hook—1 sc dec;** work in pat to last 2 sc, dec 1 sc over last 2 sc—34 (38, 42) sc. Ch 1, turn. *Rows 5-7:* Work even. *Row 8:* Rep Row 4—32 (36, 40) sc. Work 3 (3, 4) rows even. Ch 1, turn.

Next row: **Make 2 sc in first sc—1 sc inc;** work in pat to last sc, inc 1 sc in last sc—34 (38, 42) sc. Ch 1, turn. Work 2 rows even. Continuing in pat, inc 1 sc at each end of next row and every 3rd (3rd, 4th) row 3 times more. Work even over 42 (46, 50) sc until total length is 9½ (10, 10½) inches; end on wrong side. Turn.

Armhole shaping: *Row 1:* Sl st in first 2 (2, 3) sc, ch 1, sc in next 38 (42, 44) sc. Do not work over last 2 (2, 3) sc. Ch 1, turn.

Rows 2-4: Work in pat, dec 1 sc at each end of row. Ch 1, turn.

Work even over 32 (36, 38) sc until length from first row of armhole shaping is 4 (5, 6) inches. Ch 1, turn.

Next row: Inc 1 sc at each end, work across. Work even over 34 (38, 40) sc until length from first row of armhole shaping is 8 (8½, 9½) inches, end on wrong side. Turn.

Right shoulder shaping—*Row 1:* Sl st in first 4 (5, 5) sc, ch 1; sc in next 5 (6, 6) sc; dec 1 sc over next 2 sc. Do not work over rem 23 (25, 27) sc. Ch 1, turn.

Row 2: Sc in first 5 (6, 6) sc, sl st in last sc. Fasten off.

Left shoulder shaping—*Row 1:* With right side facing, skip next 12, (12, 14) sc on last long row worked; attach yarn in next sc, ch 1; dec 1 sc over first 2 sc, sc in next 5 (6, 6) sc. Do not work over rem 4 (5, 5) sc. Turn. *Row 2:* Sl st in first sc, sc in next 5 (6, 6) sc. Fasten off.

Left front: Starting at lower edge, ch 21 (23, 25) to measure approximately 8 (8½, 9½) inches.

Row 1 (right side): Sc in second ch from hook and in each ch across—20 (22, 24) sc. Mark end of row for front edge of jacket; ch 1, turn. *Rows 2-3:* Sc in each sc; ch 1, turn. *Row 4:* Work in pat, dec 1 sc at side edge only; ch 1, turn. *Rows 5-7:* Work even; ch 1, turn. *Row 8:* Rep Row 4—18 (20, 22) sc. Work even for 3 (3, 4) rows; ch 1, turn.

Continuing in pat, inc 1 sc at side edge on next row and at same edge every 3rd (3rd, 4th) row 4 times more—23 (25, 27) sc.

Armhole and collar shaping—*Row 1:* At armhole edge sl st in first 2 (2, 3) sc, sc in each sc across to last sc, inc 1 sc in last sc for shawl collar. Ch 1, turn. *Row 2:* Inc 1 sc at front edge and dec 1 sc at armhole edge, sc across. Ch 1, turn.

Rows 3-4: Rep last row twice—22 (24, 25) sts. Keeping armhole edge straight, continue in pat, inc 1 sc at front edge of every row 4 (1, 3) times more; then every other row 1 (5, 5) more times. Work 1 row even.

Next row: Inc 1 sc at each end, sc in each sc across. Keeping armhole edge even, continue incs at front edge of every other row until there are 33 (35, 37) sc. Work even until length from first row of armhole shaping is 8 (8½, 9½) inches, end at armhole edge. Turn and begin shoulder shaping as follows:

Shoulder shaping—*Row 1:* Sl st in first 4 (5, 5) sc, ch 1; sc in next 5 (6, 6) sc, dec 1 sc over next 2 sc. Do not work over rem 22 (22, 24) sc. Ch 1, turn. *Row 2:* Sc in first 5 (6, 6) sc, sl st in next sc. Turn.

Work collar as follows: Sl st in first 6 (7, 7) shoulder sts, ch 1, work even over the 22 (22, 24) sc for collar until length from last row of shoulder shaping is 2½ (2½, 3) inches. Fasten off.

Right front: Work as for left front until Row 1 has been completed, marking beg of row for front edge. Continue as for left front until Row 14 is completed, ending at front edge. Ch 1, turn.

Next row: Sc in first 3 sc; ch 2, sk next 2 sc for buttonhole; complete row. *Following row:* Sc in each sc and each ch across. Work as for left front to beg shoulder shaping, end at front edge. Ch 1, turn.

Shoulder shaping—*Row 1:* Sc in first 22 (22, 24) sc, dec 1 sc over next 2 sc, sc in fol 5 (6, 6) sc. Do not work over rem 4 (5, 5) sc. Turn. *Row 2:* Sl st in first sc, sc in each rem sc. Ch 1, turn. Now work over the first 22, (22, 24) sc only for collar until length from last row of shoulder shaping is 2½ (2½, 3) inches. Fasten off.

Sleeves: Starting at lower edge, ch 24 to measure 9½ inches.

Row 1: Sc in second ch from hook and in each ch across—23 sc. Ch 1, turn. *Rows 2-6:* Sc in each sc across row. Ch 1, turn. Inc 1 sc at each end of next row and every 14th (12th, 9th) row until there are 31 (33, 35) sc. Work even until total length is 18½ (19½, 20) inches. Turn.

Top shaping: Work as for back armhole shaping until Row 4 of armhole shaping is completed. *Next row:* Work even. *Following row:* Dec 1 st at each end, sc in each sc across.

Rep last 2 rows 5 (5, 7) times more. Work 1 row even. Turn.

Next row: Sl st across first 2 (2, 0) sts; work in pat across to last 2 (2, 0) sts. Ch 1, turn. Sc in each sc across. Fasten off.

Sew shoulder seams. Sew narrow edges of collar together. Sew collar to back of neck. Sew side and sleeve seams. Sew in sleeves, easing to fit. Turn up a 1-inch cuff on sleeves.

Button: Ch 4, sl st in first ch to form ring. *Rnd 1:* Ch 3, make 12 dc in ring, sl st in top of ch-3. *Rnd 2:* Sc in each dc, sl st in first sc. Fasten off, leaving a 10-inch length. Thread end through needle and draw through sts of last rnd. Insert button and gather tightly around button. Sew button in place.

Flap—make 2: Beg at top edge, ch 12. *Row 1:* Sc in second ch from hook and in each ch across—11 sc. Ch 1, turn. *Rows 2-4:* Sc in each sc. Ch 1, turn. At end of last row do not ch 1 to turn; sl st around outer edges of flap. Fasten off.

Sew top edge of a flap to left front 3 inches from side seam and 3½ inches from lower edge. Sew top edge of other flap to right front in same way. With right side facing, attach yarn to side seam at lower edge; being careful to keep work flat, sl st around entire outer edge. Fasten off. *Optional:* Sew shoulder pads in place.

Popcorn-Stitch Cardigan
Shown on page 53

Directions are given for size Small (8-10). Changes for sizes Medium (12-14) and Large (16-18) are in parentheses. Bust measurement = 31½-32½ (34-36, 38-40) inches.

MATERIALS

- Coats & Clark Red Heart Shetland Look Yarn, or a suitable substitute, (2-ply, 50-gram balls): 13 (15, 16) balls of No. 67 brown
- Size J crochet hook
- 8 buttons, ¾-inch diameter

Abbreviations: See pages 26-27.
Gauge: Sc pattern—3 sc = 1 inch; 10 rows = 3 inches. *Pc stitch*—2 pc sts with 3 dc between = 2 inches; 3 pc rows = 2 inches.

INSTRUCTIONS

Back, waistband: Starting at narrow edge, ch 11, having 3 ch sts per inch. *Row 1:* Sc in second ch from hook and in each ch across—10 sc. Ch 1, turn. *Row 2:* Sc in *back* loop of each sc across. Ch 1, turn. Rep last row until waistband (not stretched) is 14 (16, 18) inches. Do not turn at end of last row.

Lower back section—*Row 1:* Working along end sts of rows, ch 1, make 39 (43, 49) sc evenly spaced across next long edge to next corner. *Mark this row for right side.* Ch 1, turn. *Work sc through both loops throughout. Rows 2-3:* Sc in each sc across. Ch 1, turn.

Row 4: **Make 2 sc in first sc—inc made;** sc in each sc across to last sc, inc 1 sc in last sc—41 (45, 51) sc. Work 3 rows even. Continuing in pat, inc 1 sc at each end of next row and every fourth row 6 times more—55 (59, 65) sc. If necessary, work even until total length is 14 (14½, 14½) inches. Fasten off.

Upper back section—*Row 1:* With right side facing, attach yarn to right corner of waistband. Ch 1, sc in same place where yarn was attached. Working along other long edge of waistband, make 38 (42, 48) sc evenly spaced to next corner. Ch 1, turn. *Row 2:* Increasing 1 sc at each end, sc in each sc across—41 (45, 51) sc. Ch 1, turn.

Rows 3-4: Sc in each sc across. Ch 1, turn. Continue in pat, inc 1 sc at each end of next row and every third row 2 times more, then every other row 2 (3, 3) times. If necessary, work even over 51 (57, 63) sc until total length is 19 (19½, 20½) inches, end on wrong side; turn.

Armhole shaping—*Row 1:* Sl st across first 2 (2, 3) sts, ch 1, sc in each sc to last 2 (2, 3) sc. Ch 1, turn.

Row 2: **Draw up a loop in each of next 2 sc, yo, and draw through all 3 loops on hook—1 sc dec,** work in pat across, dec 1 sc at end of row—45 (51, 55) sc. Ch 1, turn. *Row 3:* Work even.

Continue in pat, dec 1 sc at each end of next row and every other row 2 (3, 4) times more. Work even over the 39 (43, 45) sc until length

continued

from first row of armhole shaping is 3 (3½, 4½) inches, end on wrong side. Ch 3, turn.

Work in pc st pat as follows—Row 1: Dc in next 2 (2, 1) st, **make 4 dc in fol st, drop loop from hook, insert hook from front to back in first dc of 4-dc group and draw dropped loop through, ch 1—front pc st made;** (dc in next 3 sts, pc st in fol st) 8 (9, 10) times; dc in rem 3 (3, 2) sts—9 (10, 11) pc sts and 3 (3, 2) dc at end, counting ch-3 as 1 st. Ch 3, turn.

Row 2: Dc in 0 (0, 3) sts, **(make 4 dc in fol st, drop loop from hook, insert hook back to front in first dc of the 4-dc group and draw the dropped loop through, ch 1—back pc st made;** dc in next 3 sts) 9 (10, 9) times; back pc st in next st, dc in next 0 (0, 3) sts, dc in top of turning chain—10 (11, 10) pc sts and 1 (1, 4) sts at each end. Ch 3, turn. Rep last 2 rows twice more. At end of last row, do not ch 3; turn.

Right shoulder shaping—*Row 1:* Sl st across first 6 (6, 7) sts, ch 1, sc in fol st, hdc in next st, dc in fol st, work in pat over next 4 (5, 5) sts. Do not work over rem 26 (29, 30) sts. Ch 3, turn. *Row 2:* Skip next st, work in pat over next 2 (3, 3) sts, hdc in fol dc, sc in next hdc, sl st in next st. Fasten off.

Left shoulder shaping—*Row 1:* With right side facing, skip next 13 (15, 15) sts of last long row worked for back of neck, attach yarn in next st, ch 3, work in pat over next 4 (5, 5) sts, hdc in next st, sc in next st; do not work over rem 6 (6, 7) sts. Turn. *Row 2:* Sl st in first sc, sc in next hdc, dc in fol st, work in pat to last 2 sts, skip next st, dc in top of ch-3. Fasten off.

Left front, waistband: Work as for back waistband for 6½ (7½, 8½) inches. Do not turn at end of last row.

Lower left, front section—*Row 1* (right side): Ch 1, working along end sts of rows, make 18 (20, 23) sc evenly spaced across next long edge to next corner. *Mark beg of row for front edge.* Ch 1, turn. *Rows 2-3:* Sc in each sc across. Ch 1, turn.

Row 4: Inc 1 sc at side edge, sc in each sc across—19 (21, 24) sc. Ch 1, turn. Work 3 rows even.

Continuing in pat, inc 1 st at side edge of next row and every fourth row 6 times more—26 (28, 31) sc. If necessary, work even in pat until total length is 14 (14½, 14½) inches. Fasten off.

Upper section, left front—*Row 1:* With right side of front facing, attach yarn to top right corner of waistband, ch 1, sc in same place yarn is attached. Working across other long edge of waistband, make 17 (19, 22) sc evenly spaced to next corner. Ch 1, turn.

Row 2: Work in pat across, inc 1 sc at side edge—19 (21, 24) sc. Ch 1, turn. *Rows 3-4:* Work even.

Continue to work in pat, inc 1 sc at side edge of next row and every third row twice more; then every other row 2 (3, 3) times—24 (27, 30) sc. Work even until total length is 19 (19½, 20½) inches, end at side edge. Turn.

Armhole shaping—*Row 1:* Sl st across first 2 (2, 3) sts, ch 1, complete row—22 (25, 27) sc. Ch 1, turn.

Row 2: Work across, dec 1 st at armhole edge. *Row 3:* Work even.

Continue in pat, dec 1 st at armhole edge of next row and every other row 2 (3, 4) times more. Work even over the 18 (20, 21) sc until length from first row of armhole shaping is 3 (3½, 4½) inches, end on wrong side. Ch 3, turn.

Work in pc st pat as follows—Row 1: Dc in next 2 (2, 1) sts, front pc st in next st, (dc in next 3 sts, front pc st in next st) 3 (3, 4) times; dc in last 2 (4, 2) sts—4 (4, 5) pc sts. Ch 3, turn. *Row 2:* Dc in next 3 (1, 3) sts, back pc st in next st, (dc in next 3 sts, back pc st in fol st) 3 (4, 3) times; dc in next 0 (0, 3) sts, dc in top of turning ch—4 (5, 4) pc sts. Ch 3, turn. *Rows 3-4:* Rep last 2 rows.

Neck shaping—*Row 1:* Work as for Row 1 of pc st pat to last 3 (4, 4) sts; do not work over rem sts. Ch 3, turn. *Row 2:* **Holding back on hook the last loop of each dc, dc in next 2 sts, yarn over and draw through all 3 loops on hook—1 dc decreased;** complete row in pat. Turn.

Shoulder shaping—*Row 1:* Sl st across first 6 (6, 7) sts, ch 1, sc in fol st, hdc in next st, dc in fol st, work in pat to last 2 sts, dec 1 dc over last 2 sts. Ch 3, turn.

Row 2: Rep Row 2 of right shoulder shaping of back.

Right front: Work as for the left front until Row 1 of waistband is completed. Mark last st on row for front edge. Work as for left front to neck shaping.

Neck shaping—*Row 1:* Sl st in the first 4 (5, 5) sts; ch 3, work in pat across. Ch 3, turn. *Row 2:* Work to last 2 sts, dec 1 dc over last 2 sts. Ch 3, turn.

Shoulder shapings—*Row 1:* Work in pat to last 7 (8, 8) sts, hdc in next st, sc in fol st, sl st in next st. Turn. *Row 2:* Rep Row 2 of left shoulder shaping of back.

Sleeves, cuff: Work as for waistband of back until piece (slightly stretched) measures 9 (9½, 10) inches. Do not turn at end of last row. Continue to work sleeve as follows—*Row 1:* Working along end sts of next long edge, make 27 (29, 31) sc evenly spaced across. Mark row for right side. Ch 1, turn.

Rows 2-6: Sc in each sc across. Ch 1, turn. Continue in pat, inc 1 st at each end of next row and every eighth row until there are 37 (39, 41) sc. Work even until total length is 17 (17½, 17½) inches. Turn.

Top shaping—*Row 1:* Sl st across first 2 (2, 3) sts, ch 1, work in pat to last 2 (2, 3) sts. Ch 1, turn.

Row 2: Dec 1 sc at each end, work in pat across—31 (33, 33) sts.

Row 3: Work even. Dec 1 st at each end of next row and every other row 5 (6, 6) times more—19 sts rem, end on wrong side. Ch 3, turn.

Work in pc pat as follows—Row 1: Dc in next 2 sts, front pc in next st; (dc in next 3 sts, front pc in next st) 3 times; dc in last 3 sts. Ch 3, turn. *Row 2:* Dec over next 2 sts, dc in next 2 sts, back pc in next st; (dc in next 3 sts, back pc in next st) twice; dc in next 2 st, dec over next 2 sts (sk turning ch). Ch 3, turn.

Row 3: Dec over next 2 sts, dc in next 2 sts, (front pc in next st, dc in next 3 sts) twice; dec over next 2 sts (sk turning ch). Ch 3, turn.

Row 4: Dec over next 2 sts; dc in next 3 sts, back pc in next st, dc in next 3 sts, dec over next 2 sts. Ch 3, turn.

Row 5: Dec over next 2 sts, dc in next 4 sts, dec over next 2 sts. Fasten off.

Pocket (make 2): Ch 19 to measure 6 inches. *Row 1* (right side): Dc in fourth ch from hook, front pc st in next ch, (dc in next 3 ch, front pc st in next ch) 3 times; dc in last 2 ch—4 pcs. Ch 3, turn. *Row 2:* (Dc in next 3 sts, back pc st in fol st) 3 times; dc in last 3 sts, dc in top of ch-3—3 pc sts. Ch 3, turn.

Row 3: Dc in next st, (front pc st in next st, dc in next 3 sts) 3 times; front pc st in next st, dc in next st, dc in top of turning ch. Ch 3, turn.

Rep last 2 rows 3 times. Ch 1, turn.

Top band of pocket—*Row 1:* Sc in each st across—17 sc. Ch 1, turn.

Row 2: Sc in each sc across. Fasten off. Pin pieces to measurements, dampen, and leave to dry. Sew shoulder seams.

Front and neckband: With the right side facing up, attach yarn to lower right front corner, ch 1, sc in same place yarn was attached. Being careful to keep work flat, make 73 (75, 83) sc along right front edge to next corner, 3 sc in corner, makes 37 (39, 39) sc evenly around neck to next corner, 3 sc in corner, make 73 (75, 83) sc along left front edge to next corner. Ch 1, turn.

Row 2: Sc in *back* loop of each sc across. Ch 1, turn.

Row 3: Sc in *back* loop of first 6 (7, 6) sc, ch 1, skip next sc for buttonhole, [sc in *back* loop of next 8 (8, 9) sc, ch 1, skip next sc] 7 times; sc in *back* loop of rem sc. Ch 1, turn.

Row 4: Sc in *back* loop of each sc and each ch across. Ch 1, turn.

Row 5: Sc in *back* loop of each sc across. Fasten off at end of row.

Sew side and sleeve seams. Sew in sleeves, easing to fit. Sew pockets to front as shown. Add buttons.

Man's Cardigan
Shown on page 53

Directions are for size Small (38-40); changes for sizes Medium (42-44) and Large (46-48) are in parentheses. Finished chest measurement = 43 (47, 51) inches; back width = 21 (23, 25) inches; sleeve width = 15 (16, 16) inches.

———— MATERIALS ————

- Columbia-Minerva Wool 4-ply Worsted (4-ounce skeins), or a suitable substitute: 7 (8, 8) skeins
- Size K aluminum crochet hook, or size to obtain gauge
- Size J crochet hook
- 5 buttons, ⅞-inch diameter

Abbreviations: See pages 26-27.
Gauge: 4 sts (sc, ch 1, sc, ch 1) = 1 inch; 4 rows = 1 inch.

———— INSTRUCTIONS ————

Back: Using Size K hook, ch 85 (93, 101) to measure about 21 (23, 25) inches.

Row 1: Sc in third ch from hook, * ch 1, sk ch, sc in next ch; rep from * across, ch 2, turn.

Row 2: Sc in first ch-1 sp, * ch 1, sc in next sp; rep from * across, end sc in turning ch-2 sp; ch 2, turn.

Rep Row 2 for pat. Work to 18 inches from beg or desired length to underarm. Turn, but do *not* ch 2 at end of last row.

Armholes: Ch 1, sl st in each of next 4 sts (these sts are sc, ch-1 sp, sc, and ch-1 sp); ch 2, and work in pat to last 4 sts; leave rem sts unworked. Ch 2, turn. *Next row:* Work even in pat; ch 2, turn.

Dec row: Sk first ch-1 sp, sc in next sp, work in pat across (2 sts dec at beg of row). Rep dec *every* row 5 (7, 9) times more—63 (67, 71) sts. Work even to 9 (9½, 10) inches from beg of armhole (measure in a straight line). Ch 1, turn.

Shoulders: Sl st in next 7 sts, ch 2, work pat to last 7 sts, leave rem 7 sts unworked; ch 1, turn.

Next 2 rows: Sl st in first 7 (7, 8) sts, work in pat leaving last 7 (7, 8) sts unworked. Fasten off. There are 21 (25, 25) sts for back of neck.

Left front: Ch 43 (49, 51) to measure approximately 10½ (12, 12½) inches. Work pat as for back on 41 (47, 49) sts to 1 inch less than back to underarm. Mark left edge for neck edge.

Neck and armhole: Work dec row (as for back) at neck edge of every fourth row 6 (7, 7) times, *and at the same time,* when front measures same as back to underarm, sl st across 4 sts at armhole edge, then work dec row every other row 3 (4, 5) times. After last neck edge dec, work on rem 20 (22, 22) sts to match back armhole; end at armhole edge.

Shoulder: Sl st across 6 sts, work in pat across. *Next row:* Work in pat across 8 sts, leave rem sts unworked. Fasten off.

Right front: Work same as left front, reversing shapings.

Sleeves: Ch 41 (45, 45). Work in pat on 39 (43, 43) sts for 3 inches.

Inc row: **In first ch-1 sp, work sc, ch 1, sc—2 sts inc at beg of row;** work in pat across. Rep inc row every fifth row (alternating sides of decs) 9 times more. Work even on rem 59 (63, 63) sts to 18½ inches from beginning, or ½ inch less than the desired length to the underarm.

Sleeve cap: Sl st across 4 sts, work in pat leaving last 4 sts unworked. Work 1 row even. * Work 2 dec rows, work 2 rows even; rep from * twice. Work 12 (14, 14) dec rows—15 sts.

Finishing: Sew shoulder seams. Set in sleeves; sew side and sleeve seams. With J hook, work 4 rnds sc on lower sleeve edges. On right side, beg at lower right front edge, work 2 rnds sc on front, neck, and lower edges, spacing sts to keep edges flat and working sc, ch 1, sc at each lower corner. Mark left front of cardigan for 5 buttonholes.

Next rnd: * Sc in each sc to marker, ch 2, sk 2 sc for buttonhole; rep from * 4 times, sc to end.

Next rnd: Sc in each sc around, and *at same time,* work 2 sc in each ch-2 sp of buttonhole. *Final rnd:* Work sc in each sc around. Fasten off. Weave in all ends.

Block by steaming edges lightly; do not press. Sew on buttons.

favorite designs for

AFGHANS AND PILLOWS

Crocheted afghans and pillows are favorites with everyone—to give and to receive. Whether you make them as presents for friends or for your own family and home, you can be sure your efforts and thoughtfulness will be appreciated. In this section, you'll find ten time-honored designs to stitch in blocks, with scrap yarns, from granny squares, or in other familiar, fun-to-stitch, and imaginative patterns and techniques.

A spicy patchwork of crocheted patterns, the afghan shown here is one you can work on anywhere, anytime. The square and rectangular blocks are small enough to carry comfortably wherever you go. Work the blocks in shell stitches, box stitches, and wavy patterns. Then, outline them with a deep brown edging, set them together, and trim the afghan with a matching scalloped border. Directions for all the projects in this section begin on page 70.

AFGHANS
AND PILLOWS

◆ ◆ ◆

Among the best-loved of all afghan patterns, the ripple design, *opposite,* is worked in single crochet stitches and is completely reversible.

Your bag of yarn scraps provides the makings for the multicolored throw, *above.* Make an afghan or a bedspread, depending on how many scraps you have; instructions are included for both.

The design, *below,* only *looks* complicated. It's worked in just four sections. Shell stitches give this afghan a nubby, closely woven texture.

◆ ◆ ◆

If you can work a double crochet stitch, you can make all of these pillows, *above*, and the afghan, *opposite*, as well. Each of these home furnishings accents is crafted primarily with this simple and popular stitch.

The Irish chain pillow shams, *above* (which fit standard-size pillows), were inspired by this beloved quilt pattern. Work these shams in double crochet stitches, changing colors to simulate the pieced blocks in the quilt. Trim the edges with double ruffles crocheted directly onto the pillow front.

Or, use double crochet stitches (and triple crochet, too) to create the bobble shell pillow, *top left*. This design measures 12 inches square, and the instructions include a crocheted pillow back as well as the front.

Two traditional granny square designs—one with a rose motif— make up the pillow, *top right*, and the afghan, *opposite*. Each motif is 6 inches square. Using knitting worsted-weight yarn and colors of your choice, make four squares for the pillow or 80 squares for the 48x65-inch afghan.

AFGHANS
AND PILLOWS

◆ ◆ ◆

Texture and color come alive when you crochet these large floor pillows. In deep earth tones, the patterns are reminiscent of American Indian design, one of our richest sources of traditional folk art.

Experienced crocheters will delight in showing off their skills by working a variety of stitches, including single, half double, and double crochets. In addition, nubby picots produce the robust texture and define the designs on both the Indian cross pillow, *left*, and the Indian charcoal pattern, *right*.

These pillows are worked in knitting worsted-weight yarns. Directions are included for crocheted backs or the fronts may be attached to fabric-covered pillow forms.

Patchwork Afghan
Shown on page 62

Finished size is approximately 58x72 inches.

MATERIALS

- Unger Roly Poly, or a suitable substitute: 3 (3.5-ounce) balls each of off-white (color A), yellow (B), tile (C), rust (D), and brown (E)
- Size H aluminum crochet hook

Abbreviations: See pages 26-27.

INSTRUCTIONS

Note: When changing colors, work last st of old color until 2 lps remain on hook, then finish st with new color.

Patchwork 1: With A, ch 33.

Row 1: **Make 5 dc in third ch from hook—shell made;** * sk 2 ch, sc in next ch, sk 2 ch, 5 dc in next ch. Rep from * across, ending with 5 dc in last ch—6 shells made; ch 3, turn.

Row 2: Sc in third dc of shell, * ch 2, dc in next sc, ch 2, sc in third dc of shell. Rep from * across, ending with ch 2, dc in top of turning-ch, finishing st with B; ch 3, turn.

Row 3: 5 dc (shell) in first sc, * sc in next dc, 5 dc in next sc. Rep from * across, ending with sc in top of turning ch; ch 3, turn.

Row 4: Rep Row 2.

Rep Rows 3 and 4 for pat in the following color sequence, working Rows 3 and 4 of each color: * 2 rows C, 2 rows D, 2 rows E, 2 rows A, 2 rows B. Rep from * until there are 48 rows from beg (24 color stripes), ending with 2 rows D. Fasten off.

Border: Attach E in any corner and work around entire piece as follows: 85 sc along each long edge, 28 sc along each short edge and 3 sc in each corner. Join with a sl st to first sc. Fasten off.

Patchwork 2: Make 4 pieces as for Patchwork 1 for 32 rows (16 color stripes) in the same color sequence. Beg with A and end with A. Fasten off.

Border: Attach E and work around entire piece as follows: 57 sc along each long edge, 28 sc along each short edge and 3 sc in each corner. Fasten off.

Patchwork 3: Make 4, using colors A and B. With A, ch 31.

Row 1: Sc in second ch from hook, sc in next ch, * hdc in next ch, dc in next ch, trc in next ch, dc in next ch, hdc in next ch, sc in each of next 2 ch. Rep from * across, ending with sc in each of last 2 ch and finishing last st with B; ch 4, turn.

Row 2: Sk first st, trc in next st, * dc in next st, hdc in next st, sc in next st, hdc in next st, dc in next st, trc in next 2 sts. Rep from * across; ch 4, turn.

Row 3: Rep Row 2 with B, finishing last st with A in top of ch-4; ch 1, turn.

Row 4: * Sc in each of 2 sts, hdc in next st, dc in next st, trc in next st, dc in next st, hdc in next st. Rep from * across, ending with sc in each of 2 sts; ch 1, turn.

Row 5: Rep Row 4 with A, finishing last st with B; ch 3, turn.

Rep Rows 2-5 for pat until there are 16 rows in all, ending with 1 row of A. Fasten off.

Border: Attach E and work 28 sc around the 4 edges, working 3 sc in each corner. Fasten off.

Patchwork 4: Make 4. Work as for Patchwork 3, with colors A and C; work border with E as for Patchwork 3.

Patchwork 5: Make 4. Work as for Patchwork 3, with colors D and B; work border with E as for Patchwork 3.

Patchwork 6: Make 4. Work as for Patchwork 3, with colors A and D; work border with E as for Patchwork 3.

Patchwork 7: Make 2. Work as for Patchwork 3, with colors A and E; work border with E as for Patchwork 3.

Patchwork 8: Make 2. With E, ch 92.

Row 1: Dc in fourth ch from hook, dc in next ch—3 dc made, counting turning-ch as 1 dc; * finish last dc with C. (*Note:* Carry yarn along and work over yarn not in use.) With C, work dc in next 3 ch, finish last dc with E; with E, work dc in next 3 ch. Rep from * across—90 dc, counting turning-ch as 1 dc; end 3 dc worked with C; finish last dc with E, ch 3, turn.

Row 2: With E, work dc in next 2 sts, * changing colors as cited in Row 1, work 3 dc with C, 3 dc with E. Rep from * across, end with 3 dc with C; finish last dc with E, ch 3, turn.

Note: Always alternate colors and work 3 dc of E over 3 dc of C and 3 dc of C over 3 dc of E.

Rep Row 2 until there are 13 rows in all. Attach E, and working around patchwork piece, work 90 sc along each wide edge, 28 sc along each short edge, and 3 sc in each corner. Join with sl st to first sc. Fasten off.

Patchwork 9: Make 4. With A, ch 56.

Row 1: 3 dc in third ch from hook, * sk 2 ch, 3 dc in next ch. Rep from * across, ending with sk 1 ch, dc in last ch, finish last dc with D—eighteen 3-dc grps; ch 3, turn.

Row 2: * Skip next 3-dc grp, and still working in the foundation ch, work 3 dc in the second skipped ch. Rep from * across, ending with dc in turning-ch-lp, finish last dc with B—seventeen 3-dc grps; ch 3, turn.

Row 3: With B, work 3 dc in second dc of first dc-grp in Row 1; * 3 dc in second dc of next dc-grp in Row 1. Rep from * across, ending with dc in turning-ch-lp, finish last dc with A—eighteen 3 dc-grps; ch 3, turn.

Note: Yarn now is attached at both ends and always will be available to begin the next row as the patchwork piece continues.

Row 4: With A, work 3 dc in second dc of first dc-grp of Row 2; * 3 dc in second dc of next dc-grp in Row 2. Rep from * across, ending with dc in turning-ch-lp, finish last dc with D; ch 3, turn.

Row 5: With D, work 3 dc in second dc of first dc-grp of Row 3; * 3 dc in second dc of next dc-grp of Row 3. Rep from * across, ending with dc in turning-ch-lp, finish last dc with B; ch 3, turn.

Row 6: With B, work 3 dc in second dc of first dc-grp of Row 4; * 3 dc in second dc of next dc-grp of Row 4. Rep from * across, ending with dc in turning-ch-lp, finish last dc with A; ch 3, turn.

Continue to work pat in this manner with color sequence of A-D-B until there are 21 rows in all (7 of each color).

Border: With E, working around entire patchwork piece, work 60 sc along each wide edge, 28 sc along each short edge, and 3 sc in each corner. Join with sl st to first sc. Fasten off.

Patchwork 10: Make 4. With C, ch 31.

Row 1: Sc in second ch from hook, sc in each of next 2 ch, * dc in each of next 3 ch, sc in each of next 3 ch. Rep from * across, ending with dc in each of last 3 ch, finish last dc with B—30 sts; ch 1, turn.

Row 2: With B * sc in each of 3 dc, dc in each of 3 sc. Rep from * across, finish last dc with E; ch 1, turn.

Row 3: With E, work same as Row 2, finish last dc with C; ch 1, turn.

Row 4: With C, work same as Row 2.

Repeat Row 2 for pat in C-B-E sequence, always working sc over dc and dc over sc for 38 rows in all. Fasten off.

Border: Attach E, and working around patchwork piece, work 58 sc along long edge, 28 sc along each short edge, and 3 sc in each corner. Join with sl st to first sc. Fasten off.

Patchwork 11: Make 2. Work same as for Patchwork 10 in colors A-B-D.

Patchwork 12: Make 4. Work as for Patchwork 2 in colors E and C. Beg with E, ch and work first 2 rows E. Work E around all sides as for Patchwork 2.

Finishing: Whipstitch all pieces together with E, following chart, *below,* for placement.

3 AB	E D C B A 2	4 AC	11 ADB	4 AC	2 E D C B A	3 AB
10 CBE	5 DB A	12 EC	7 AE	12 EC	A 5 DB	10 CBE
9 ADB	6 AD	E D C B A 1	6 AD	9 ADB
8 EC	8 EC
9 ADB	6 AD	6 AD	9 ADB
10 CBE	5 DB E D C B A 2	12 EC	11 ADB	12 EC	2 E D C B A 5 DB	10 CBE
3 AB	4 AC	4 AC	3 AB

Color Key 1 Square = 1 Inch
A—Off White   C—Tile
B—Yellow   D—Rust   E—Brown
Numbers identify patchwork patterns.

Trim: Attach E in any corner. *Row 1:* Ch 1, work sc around, having same number of sts on corresponding sides and working 3 sc in each corner. Make sure all work lies flat. Join with sl st to first sc.

Row 2: Ch 1, * sk 2 sts, sc in next st, ch 1, 3 dc back in same st as sc. Rep from * around. Join with sl st to first sc. Fasten off.

Ripple Afghan
Shown on page 64

Finished size of afghan shown is approximately 46x68 inches.

──────── **MATERIALS** ────────
- Unger Roly Poly (3.5-ounce balls), or a suitable substitute: 8 balls of No. 8841 natural, 2 balls each of Nos. 7090 blue, 9381 pink, 2765 green, 8825 gold, and 8468 maroon
- Size G aluminum crochet hook, or size to obtain gauge

Abbreviations: See pages 26-27.
Gauge: 9 sc = 2 inches.

──────── **INSTRUCTIONS** ────────
With natural, ch 301.

Row 1: Sc in second st from hook, sk next st, sc in next 10 sts; * 3 sc in next st, sc in next 11 sts, skip 2 sts, sc in next 11 sts. Rep from * across 10 times more. End row with 3 sc in next sc, sc in next 10 sts, sk next st, sc in last st; ch 1, turn.

Row 2: Sc in first sc, skip next sc, working in back lp only, sc in next 10 sts; * 3 sc in next st, sc in next 11 sts, skip 2 sts, sc in next 11 sts; rep from * across 10 times more; end row with 3 sc in next sc, sc in next 10 sc, sk next sc, working under both lps sc in last sc; ch 1, turn.

Repeat Row 2 for entire afghan.

Work 8 more rows with natural. Then work stripe pat as follows: 3 rows of blue, 2 rows of natural, 3 rows of pink, 2 rows of natural, 3 rows of green, 2 rows of natural, 3 rows of gold, 2 rows of natural, 3 rows of maroon, 10 rows of natural. Rep the stripe pat 5 times more. Fasten off.

Striped Scrap Afghan
Shown on page 65

Instructions below are for a bedspread that measures 98 inches square. Changes for a smaller afghan (48x60 inches) follow in parentheses.

MATERIALS
- Approximately 120 ounces of scrap worsted-weight yarn in 20-25 colors
- Size I aluminum crochet hook, or size to obtain gauge

Abbreviations: See pages 26-27.
Gauge: 3 sc = 1 inch.

INSTRUCTIONS
Note: To change colors, work last sc of old color until 2 lps remain on hook, then finish st with new color.

With any color, ch 265 (105).

Row 1: Sc in second ch and in each ch across; change yarn in last sc of row. Break off old yarn; with new color ch 1, turn.

Row 2: Sc in each sc across, change color at end of row as for Row 1; ch 1, turn.

Rep Row 2 until work measures 88 (50) inches. Do not break off.

Border: Rep Row 2 once more across row, make 3 sc in last st; working along the long side, sc in end of each row to beg ch, 3 sc in corner st; work next 2 sides to correspond, making 3 sc in each corner, join with sl st to beg sc. Break off yarn.

Next rnd: Sc in each sc across to next corner, 3 sc in corner sc, * **draw up a lp in each of next 2 sts, yo, draw through 3 lps on hook—decrease (dec) made;** sc in each of next 4 sts. Rep from * to corner, work 3 sc in corner, sc along other end, 3 sc in corner; rep from * once more to corner, 3 sc in corner, sl st in beg sc.

Following rnd: * Working 3 sc in corners, sc around. Rep from * around until border measures 5 inches, or work reaches floor when placed on bed. Fasten off and weave in all ends.

Bobble Shell Afghan
Shown on page 65

Finished size is approximately 50x70 inches.

MATERIALS
- Talon-American Dawn Sayelle knitting worsted (4-ounce skeins), or a suitable substitute: 3 skeins each of Nos. 311 green and 326 red, 6 skeins of No. 329 rust, 2 skeins of No. 362 purple, and 1 skein No. 324 maroon
- Size G aluminum crochet hook

Abbreviations: See pages 26-27.

INSTRUCTIONS
Note: This afghan has four sections. Each section is worked separately, then all four are stitched together.

Section: With maroon, ch 52.

Row 1: 2 dc in fourth ch from hook, sk 2 ch, sc in next ch; * **ch 2, 2 dc in same ch as last sc—shell made;** sk 2 ch, sc in next ch. Rep from * across, ending with sc in last ch; ch 3, turn—16 shells.

Row 2: 2 dc in first sc, **sc in ch-2 lp, * ch 2, 2 dc in same ch-2 lp—shell made;** sc in next ch-2 lp. Rep from * across, ending with sc in last ch-2 lp; ch 3, turn. Rep Row 2 three times more. Work should measure about 2¼x14 inches. Do not ch 3 at end of Row 5. Break off yarn.

Row 6: Attach green in same sp as last sc, ch 3, turn, work in pat across row; in last ch-2 lp work shell, do not turn, sc in same sp, ch 2, 2 dc in same sp—corner made; sc over turning ch-3 of Row 3, ch 2, 2 dc in same sp; sc in same ch used to make first shell in Row 1; ch 3, turn.

Row 7: 2 dc in first sc, work shell in each of next 2 ch-2 lps; in next ch-2 lp make 2 shells; continue across row and work 15 more shells; sc in last ch-2 lp; ch 3, turn.

Row 8: 2 dc in first sc, work 16 shells across row, in next ch-2 lp make 2 shells; work shell in each of next 2 ch-2 lps, sc in turning-ch; ch 3, turn.

Row 9: 2 dc in first sc, work shell in each of next 3 ch-2 lps; in next ch-2 lp make 2 shells; work in pat across row.

Work in pat as established, and at the same time, on each row, increase 1 shell on each of the 2 sides and work 2 shells in the corner ch-2 lp. Work 1 more row with green; fasten off.

Continue in pat with 5 rows of red; 5 rows of rust; 2 rows each of purple, rust, red, green, red, green, red, rust, and purple; 5 rows each of rust, red, and green. Do not break off; ch 1, turn. Sc in first sc, sc around the same 2 sides, working sc's in the second dc of each shell, in the ch-2 sp's, and in each sc. Break off—1 section made.

Work 3 more sections as given above. With green yarn, whipstitch sections together, working through both lps of the sc's.

Border: Join rust in any ch-3 lp, ch 3, and work a row of shells around entire afghan; join with sc in first ch-3 lp; ch 3, turn.

Continue to work shells around afghan for 6 more rnds and inc in each corner by working 2 shells in ch-2 lp of corner shell, join with sc in first ch-3 lp; ch 3, turn. Break yarn and work as established 2 rows of shells in purple.

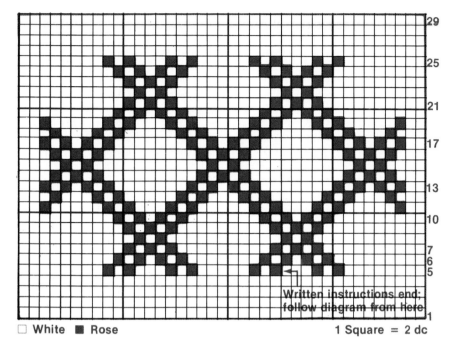

29
25
21
17
13
10
7
6
5

1

Written instructions end; follow diagram from here

☐ White ■ Rose

1 Square = 2 dc

Irish Chain Pillow Sham

Shown on page 66

Finished size of each pillow is 20x26 inches, excluding ruffle. The sham will fit a standard-size bed pillow.

MATERIALS

- Bernat Sesame 4-ply knitting worsted (3.5-ounce balls), or a suitable substitute: 4 balls of white, 3 balls of rosewood
- Size H aluminum crochet hook, or size to obtain gauge
- Fabric to cover back of sham

Abbreviations: See pages 26-27.
Gauge: 4 dc = 1 inch; 3 rows = 1¾ inches.

INSTRUCTIONS

Note: To change yarn colors, work last st of old color until 2 lps remain on hook, then finish st with new color. This pattern allows you to work over the color not in use to avoid fastening off after each color change in a row. Exceptions to this are the 3 rows in the center of each diamond shape, where the distance between color changes is greater.

After working the final stitch of the second color in each row, drop that color and pick it up again in the next row where it is needed. Do not carry it across and back.

With white yarn, ch 80.

Row 1: Dc in fourth ch from hook and in each ch across; ch 3, turn—78 dc.

Row 2: Dc in second dc and in each dc across row; ch 3, turn.

Rows 3-4: Rep Row 2.

Row 5: (Turning ch counts as first dc), dc in second dc and in next 14 dc, finish last dc with rosewood, dc in each of next 2 dc; change to white, dc in each of next 2 dc; with rosewood, dc in next 2 dc; with white, dc in each of next 6 dc. Using the diagram, *above,* begin work as indicated with arrow, and work 2 dc for each square in the grid. Dc in each dc for 29 rows total. Fasten off.

Border: *Rnd 1:* With right side facing, attach rosewood in beg of last row worked, ch 3, dc in each dc across row to corner, in corner st work (2 dc, ch 2, 2 dc); work 2 dc over each end st of each row to next corner; work corner as before and continue around, ending with 2 dc, ch 2, dc in beg st; join with sl st to top of beg ch-3.

Rnd 2: Rep Rnd 1, ending with 2 dc, ch 2, 2 dc in corner sp; join with sl st to top of beg ch-3.

Rnds 3-4: With white, rep Rnd 1. Carefully block the pillow front to measure 20x26 inches.

Assembly: From the fabric of your choice, cut a backing piece that is the same size as the blocked pillow front. (Add seam allowance.) Press the seam allowance under and pin the backing to the back of the crocheted front, wrong sides facing.

Hand-sew three sides together, leaving one short end open for inserting the pillow. Do not sew through the last row of crochet stitches; the ruffle will be worked into these stitches.

Large ruffle: *Rnd 1* (work in back lps only for this rnd): Attach rosewood in any corner ch (the ch just to the right of first dc), ch 3, dc in same st, * 2 dc in next dc, dc in next dc. Rep from * to corner ch-2 lp; work 2 dc in first ch of corner, ch 2, 2 dc in next ch of corner. Continue around, making incs and corners as established, ending with 2 dc in corner ch, ch 2, join to the top of the beg ch-3.

Rnd 2 (work this and rem rnds of large ruffle through both lps): Ch 3, * dc in each dc to next ch-2 corner lp; in corner lp work 2 dc, ch 2, 2 dc. Rep from * around, ending with 2 dc, ch 2, 2 dc in corner sp; join with sl st to top of ch-3.

continued

Rnds 3-4: Rep Rnd 2, ending with corner as before; join to top of ch-3.

Rnd 5: Ch 5, sk 2 dc, sc in next dc, * ch 4, sk 2 dc, sc in next dc. Rep from * to corner. In corner ch-2 sps work (sc, ch 4) twice. Continue around as established. End rnd with sl st in first ch of ch-5 at the beg of the rnd.

Small ruffle: *Rnd 1* (work this rnd in the front lps only): Attach white yarn in the front lp of the same ch where the large ruffle was started; ch 3, dc in same st, * dc in next front lp, 2 dc in following front lp. Rep from * to corner; in corner ch-2 work 2 dc in first ch, ch 2, 2 dc in next ch.

Continue around, making incs and corners as established. End with 2 dc in corner ch, ch 2, sl st to the top of the beg ch-3.

Rnd 2: Work same as for Rnd 2 of large ruffle.

Rnd 3: Work same as for Rnd 5 of large ruffle. Fasten off.

Bobble Shell Pillow

Shown on page 66

Finished pillow is 12½ inches square.

MATERIALS

- Bernat Sesame 4-ply knitting worsted, or a suitable substitute: 1 (3.5-ounce) ball each of white, blue, and ocher
- Size G aluminum crochet hook, or size to obtain gauge
- ⅜ yard of fabric to cover pillow form
- 12-inch-square pillow form

Abbreviations: See pages 26-27.
Gauge: 1 colored bobble from sc to sc = 1½ inches; 1 row = 1 inch.

INSTRUCTIONS

Note: To change colors, work the last st of the old color until 2 lps remain on the hook, then finish the st with the new color.

With white yarn, ch 51.

Row 1: Sc in the fourth ch from the hook, sc in each ch across, finish the last sc with ocher yarn; ch 4, turn.

Row 2: With ocher yarn, work 2 dc in the first sc, * sk 2 sc, sc in next sc, sk 2 sc, in next sc work (2 dc, ch 1, trc, ch 1, 2 dc). Rep from * across, ending with 2 dc and trc in the turning-ch-lp, finish the last trc with white yarn; ch 1, turn.

Row 3: Sc in trc, * in next sc, work 2 dc, ch 1, trc, ch 1, 2 dc; sc in the next trc. Rep from * across, ending with sc in the turning-ch-lp, finish the last sc with blue yarn; ch 4, turn.

Row 4: 2 dc in first sc, * sc in trc, in the next sc work 2 dc, ch 1, trc, ch 1, 2 dc. Rep from * across, ending with 2 dc and trc in last sc, finish the last trc with white yarn; ch 1, turn.

Rep Rows 3 and 4, always working Row 3 in white yarn and Row 4 alternately in blue and ocher yarns, until there is a total of 13 blue and ocher rows, ending with ocher and changing to white. Ch 1, turn.

Last row: Sc in each st across the row, omitting ch-1 at the end of the row. Fasten off.

Border: With right side facing (white rows are indented), attach blue yarn in the corner ch at the beg of the last row worked; ch 3, work dc in each sc and dc evenly along the ends of the rows, working 3 dc in each corner. Join with sl st to the ch-3 at the beg of the rnd.

Finishing: Press and block the finished pillow front to 12½ inches square. Cut and stitch the fabric to cover the pillow form, leaving one side open. Turn and press. Tack the crocheted piece to one side; insert the pillow form, and sew the remaining side closed.

Granny Square Pillow

Shown on page 66

Finished pillow is 12½ inches square.

MATERIALS

- Bernat Sesame 4-ply knitting worsted, or a suitable substitute: 1 (3.5-ounce) skein each of blue, olive green, white, rosewood, and ocher
- Size G aluminum crochet hook, or size to obtain gauge
- ⅜ yard of fabric to cover pillow form
- 12-inch-square pillow form

Abbreviations: See pages 26-27.
Gauge: One square = 5¾ inches square, before blocking.

INSTRUCTIONS

Rose motif: Make 2. With ocher, ch 5, join with sl st to form ring.

Rnd 1 (right side): Ch 1, sc in ring, * ch 5, sc in ring. Rep from * 7 times more; join last ch-5 with sl st to first sc—8 lps made. Fasten off.

Rnd 2: With wrong side facing, attach rosewood yarn by putting the hook through the center ring and drawing a lp through, securing st on base ring (between 2 sc on Rnd 1). * Ch 6, sk next 2 sc, sl st between next 2 sc. Rep from * around; join last ch-6 with sl st to first ch; ch 1, turn—4 ch-6 lps made.

Rnd 3: * Sc in next ch-6 lp, in same lp work (7 dc, sc). Rep from * around—4 petals made; join with sl st to sc at beg of rnd. Fasten off.

Rnd 4: With wrong side facing, attach ocher around bar of fourth dc of first petal * ch 7, sl st around bar of fourth dc of next petal. Rep from * 3 times more; join with sl st to beg bar; ch 1, turn.

Rnd 5: In first ch-7 lp and in each lp around work (sc, hdc, 4 dc, hdc, sc). Join with sl st to first sc; do not turn.

Rnd 6: * Ch 6, sk hdc, sl st in next dc, ch 6, sk 2 dc, sl st in next dc, ch 6, sk 2 sts, sl st in next sc. Rep from * around; join last ch-6 in sl st at beg of rnd. Fasten off—12 ch-6 lps.

Rnd 7: (*Note:* This rnd will leave lps made in Rnd 6 unworked. Crochet only in sts of Rnd 5. Bend lps forward to work.) With the right side facing, join olive yarn in hdc directly left of where the last rnd was fastened off, in the same st work (ch 4, 2 trc), ch 2, * sk dc where sl st was made, in the next dc work 2 dc, dc in next dc, ch 2, 2 trc in next hdc, trc in next sc, ch 3—corner ch made; in the next hdc work 3 trc, ch 2. Rep from * around, end with ch 3; sl st to the top of the beg ch-4. Fasten off.

Rnd 8: Attach white yarn in any ch-3 corner sp, ch 3; in same sp work 2 dc, ch 3, 3 dc, * ch 1, (in next ch-2 sp work 3 dc, ch 1) twice; in next corner sp work (3 dc, ch 3, 3 dc). Rep from * around, ending with ch 1; sl st in top of ch-3. Fasten off.

Rnd 9: Attach blue yarn in any corner sp, ch 3, in the same sp work 2 dc, ch 3, 3 dc; ch 1, * (in the next ch-1 sp work 3 dc, ch 1) 3 times. In the next corner sp work (3 dc, ch 3, 3 dc); ch 1. Rep from * around, ending with ch 1; join with sl st to the top of the beg ch-3. Fasten off.

Granny motif: Make 2. With rosewood, ch 6, sl st to form ring.
Rnd 1: Ch 3, 2 dc in ring, ch 3, * 3 dc in ring, ch 3. Rep from * 2 times more, ending with sl st in top of beg ch-3. Fasten off.

Rnd 2: Attach ocher yarn in any ch-3 sp, ch 3, in the same sp work 2 dc, ch 3, 3 dc; * ch 2, in the next ch-3 sp work (3 dc, ch 3, 3 dc). Rep from * around, ending with ch 2, sl st in the top of the beg ch-3. Fasten off.

Rnd 3: Attach light olive yarn in any ch-3 corner sp, ch 3, in the same sp work 2 dc, ch 3, 3 dc, * ch 2, in the next sp work 3 dc; ch 2, in the corner sp, (work 3 dc, ch 3, 3 dc).

Rep from * around, ending with ch 2; sl st in the top of the beg ch-3. Fasten off.

Rnd 4: Attach white yarn in any corner sp, ch 3, in the same sp work 2 dc, ch 3, 3 dc, * ch 1, (in the next ch-2 sp work 3 dc, ch 1) 2 times; in the corner sp work (3 dc, ch 3, 3 dc). Rep from * around; ch 1, sl st in the top of the beg ch-3. Fasten off.

Rnd 5: Attach blue yarn and work same as for Rnd 4, except rep between ( )s 3 times. Fasten off.

Pillow: Block the squares to 5¾x5¾ inches. Arrange them with roses and granny squares in the opposite corners. With blue yarn and the wrong sides of the square facing each other, sl st the 4 squares together in the back lps only.

Border: Working in the back lps, attach blue yarn in the center ch of any ch-3 corner, ch 3, dc in the same ch, * dc in each st across the row to the corner. In the center ch of ch-3 corner work 2 dc, ch 2, 2 dc. Rep from * around, ending with 2 dc in beg st, ch 2, sl st in the top of the ch-3.

Finishing: Press and block the finished pillow front to 12½ inches square. Sew together the fabric to cover the pillow form on three sides; tack the crocheted piece to one side. Insert the pillow form, and sew the remaining side closed.

Granny Square and Rose Afghan
Shown on page 67

Finished size is approximately 48x60 inches.

———— MATERIALS ————
• Unger Roly Poly (3.5-ounce skeins), or a suitable substitute: 4 skeins of blue, 3 skeins each of green and white, and 2 skeins each of light gold and gold
• Size G aluminum crochet hook, or size to obtain gauge

Abbreviations: See pages 26-27.
Gauge: One square = 5¾x5¾ inches, before blocking.

———— INSTRUCTIONS ————
Rose square: Make 28. With gold yarn, ch 5, join with sl st to form a ring.

Rnd 1 (right side): Ch 1, sc in ring, * ch 5, sc in ring. Rep from * 7 times more; join last ch-5 with sl st to first sc—8 lps made. Fasten off.

Rnd 2: With the wrong side facing, attach light gold yarn by putting the hook through the center ring and drawing a lp through, securing the st on the base ring (between 2 sc on Rnd 1); * ch 6, sk next 2 sc, sl st between the next 2 sc. Rep from * around; join last ch-6 with sl st to the first ch; ch 1, turn—4 ch-6 lps made.

Rnd 3: * Sc in next ch-6 lp, in the same lp work (7 dc, sc). Rep from * around—4 petals made; join with sl st to sc at the beg of the rnd. Fasten off.

Rnd 4: With wrong side facing, attach gold yarn around bar of the fourth dc of the first petal, * ch 7, sl st around the bar of the fourth dc of the next petal. Rep from * around 3 times more; join with sl st around the beg bar; ch 1, turn.

Rnd 5: In the first ch-7 lp and in each loop around work (sc, hdc, 4 dc, hdc, sc). Join with sl st to the first sc. Do not turn.

Rnd 6: * Ch 6, sk hdc, sl st in the next dc, ch 6, sk 2 dc, sl st in next dc, ch 6, sk next 2 sts, sl st in next sc. Rep from * around; join last ch-6 in sl st at the beg of the rnd. Fasten off—12 ch-6 lps made.

Rnd 7: Note—This rnd will leave the lps made in Rnd 6 unworked; work only in the sts of Rnd 5. Bend the lps forward to work. With the right side facing, join green yarn in the hdc directly left of where the last rnd was fastened off, in same st work (ch 4, 2 trc), ch 2, * sk dc where sl st was made, in next dc work 2 dc, dc in next dc, ch 2, 2 trc in next hdc, trc in next sc, ch 3—corner ch made; 3 trc in next hdc, ch 2. Rep from * around, ending with ch 3, sl st to the top of the beg ch-4. Fasten off.

continued

Rnd 8: Attach white yarn in any ch-3 corner sp, ch 3, in the same sp work 2 dc, ch 3, 3 dc. * Ch 1, (in the next ch-2 sp work 3 dc, ch 1) twice; in the corner sp work (3 dc, ch 3, 3 dc). Rep from * around, ending with ch 1; sl st in the top of the beg ch-3. Fasten off.

Rnd 9: Attach blue yarn in any corner sp, ch 3, in the same sp work 2 dc, ch 3, 3 dc. Ch 1, * (in the next ch-1 sp work 3 dc, ch 1) 3 times; in the next corner sp work (3 dc, ch 3, 3 dc), ch 1. Rep from * around, ending with ch 1, sl st in the top of the beg ch-3. Fasten off.

Granny motif (make 52): With light gold, ch 6, join with sl st to form ring.

Rnd 1: Ch 3, 2 dc in ring, ch 3, * 3 dc in ring, ch 3. Rep from * 2 times more, end with sl st in top of beg ch-3. Fasten off.

Rnd 2: Attach gold yarn in any corner ch-3 sp; ch 3, in the same sp work 2 dc, ch 3, 3 dc; * ch 2, in the next sp work (3 dc, ch 3, 3 dc); ch 2, rep from * around, ending with ch 2, sl st to the top of the beg ch-3. Fasten off.

Rnd 3: Attach green yarn in any corner sp, ch 3, in the same sp work 2 dc, ch 3, 3 dc; * ch 2, in the next sp work 3 dc; ch 2, in the corner sp work (3 dc, ch 3, 3 dc). Rep from * around, ending with ch 2, sl st in the top of the beg ch-3. Fasten off.

Rnd 4: Attach white yarn in any corner sp, ch 3, in the same sp work 2 dc, ch 3, 3 dc; * ch 1, (in the next ch-2 sp work 3 dc, ch 1) twice; in the corner sp work (3 dc, ch 3, 3 dc). Rep from * around, ending with ch 1, sl st to the top of the ch-3 at beg of round. Fasten off.

Rnd 5: With blue yarn, work as for Rnd 4, except rep between ( )s 3 times. Fasten off.

Assembly: Block the squares to approximately 6x6 inches. Do not press the rose motifs flat; the lps formed in Rnd 6 may be opened and pressed lightly.

Position 4 rose squares into a larger square for the center of the afghan. Arrange 12 granny squares around the rose squares; then place 4 more granny squares along the top and bottom edges of the assembly (8 more squares are used for this). Place a round of rose squares around the entire assembly (18 more squares used). Finally, place a round of granny squares around the entire outer edge (24 more granny squares used). The finished afghan is 8 squares wide and 10 squares long.

To join, hold the squares so the right sides are together, and with blue yarn sl st in the back lps only. Make 8 strips with 10 squares in each strip, then sl st the strips tog.

Border: Attach blue yarn in any ch-3 corner sp, ch 3, in the same sp work 2 dc, ch 3, 3 dc; * dc in each st across the row to the corner; in the corner work (3 dc, ch 3, 3 dc). Rep from * around; end with sl st to the top of the beg ch-3. Fasten off. Block the border.

Indian Cross Pillow

Shown on page 68

Materials listed below are for a crocheted front tacked to a fabric pillow. For a crocheted pillow back, purchase three additional skeins of brown yarn, and follow directions at the end of these instructions for crocheting the back.

———— MATERIALS ————

- Brunswick Germantown Knitting Worsted, or a suitable substitute: 3 (3.5-ounce) skeins of brown; 1 ounce each of rust, light brown, and purple; 2 ounces each of orange and gold; and 3 ounces of blue
- Size G crochet hook, or size to obtain gauge
- 2 yards of 36-inch-wide lining fabric for pillow
- 2 bags of polyester fiberfill

Abbreviations: See pages 26-27.
Gauge: 4 sts = 1 inch.

———— INSTRUCTIONS ————

Pillow top: Beg at center with rust, ch 4; join with sl st to form ring.

Rnd 1: Ch 1, work 12 sc in ring; join with sl st to first sc. Fasten off.

Rnd 2: Attach orange yarn in any sc, ch 2, hdc in next sc, **(3 hdc in next sc—corner made;** hdc in each of next 2 sc) 3 times; 3 hdc in last sc. Join to top of ch-2 at beg of rnd—20 hdc—4 corners.

Rnd 3: Attach brown yarn to center hdc of any corner-hdc group, ch 1, 3 sc in same place where yarn was attached, * sc in next 4 hdc, 3 sc in corner hdc. Rep from * around. Join to first sc—28 sc.

Rnd 4: Ch 1, sc in same st as join, (3 sc in corner sc, sc in each sc to next corner sc) 3 times; 3 sc in corner sc, sc in rem sc. Join—36 sc.

Rnd 5: Ch 1, sc in same st as join, (sc in each sc to corner st, 3 sc in corner sc) 4 times; sc in rem sc. Join—44 sc. Fasten off.

Rnd 6: Attach rust yarn in any sc bet corners, and rep Rnd 5.

Rnd 7: Attach light brown yarn in any sc bet corners, ch 2 (to count as first hdc); work hdc in each st around and work 3 hdc in center st of each corner; join with sl st to top of ch-2 at beg of rnd. Fasten off.

Rnd 8: Attach brown yarn in any corner st, ch 1, work 3 sc in same corner st. Work sc in each st around and at same time continue to work 3 sc in each corner st. Join to the first sc.

Rnds 9-13: Ch 1, sc in the same st as the join. Work as for Rnd 8. Fasten off at end of Rnd 13—24 sts on each side plus 3 sts at each corner—108 sts.

Side square: With pins, mark off the center 6 sts on 1 side edge. Attach brown yarn to first pin-marked st.

Row 1: Ch 1, sc in same st, sc in next 5 sts. Ch 1, turn.

Rows 2-6: Sc in 6 sc. Ch 1, turn. At the end of Row 6, fasten off. Make a side square on 3 rem side edges.

Crochet around the entire piece as follows:

Rnd 1: Attach brown yarn to any corner st on Rnd 13; ch 1; * 3 sc in the same corner st, sc in each st to the base of the side square, working along the outer edges of the square, make sc in the ends of the next 5 rows, 3 sc in the corner sc, sc in 4 sc, 3 sc in last sc, sc in the ends of next 5 rows; sc in each st to next corner st on Rnd 13. Rep from * around. Join to first sc.

Rnd 2: Attach rust yarn to the right-hand corner st on a side square, ch 2, 2 hdc in the corner st; * hdc in each st to next corner st, 3 hdc in corner st, hdc in each st to within 1 st before base of square, **(draw up a lp in next st) 3 times; yo and draw through all 4 lps on hook—dec made;** hdc in each st to next corner st, 3 hdc in corner st, hdc in each st to within 1 st before base of next square, make a dec, hdc in each st to next corner st on side square, 3 hdc in corner st. Rep from * around. Join to top of ch-2. Fasten off.

Rnd 3: With light brown yarn, work same as for Rnd 2 above. Fasten off.

Rnd 4: Attach orange yarn to a right-hand corner st on a side square, ch 1, and work as for Rnd 2 above, except make sc (instead of hdc) and make a picot after every fifth sc. **To make a picot: Ch 4, sl st in fourth ch from hook;** be sure to count all incs and decs.

Rnd 5: Attach gold yarn to right-hand corner st on side square, ch 2, 2 hdc in corner st, holding picots down on right side, hdc in each st to center st on this square; * **ch 13, hdc in third ch from hook, hdc in next 10 ch—arm made;** hdc in next st and continue as for Rnd 2 across to center of *opposite side square.* Rep from * to the end of the rnd—2 arms made. Join; fasten off.

Work short rows along half of edge as follows:

Row 1: Attach gold yarn to center st of first point to the left of an arm, ch 2, hdc in same place, work hdc across, increasing and decreasing as before to the corresponding point on the opposite edge, ending with 2 hdc in center st. Fasten off.

Row 2: Attach blue yarn to the top of the ch-2 at the beg of the last row, ch 2, hdc in the same place; then, increasing and decreasing as before, and making a picot after every fifth st, work as for the last row. Fasten off.

Row 3: Attach light brown yarn to the first st on the arm preceding the beg of the last 2 rows. Ch 2, hdc in each st of the arm, then increasing and decreasing as before, and holding picots down on the right side, work hdc across, ending with hdc in each st of the opposite arm. Fasten off.

Row 4: Attach purple yarn to the dec at the base of the arm, ch 1, sc in the same place, making a picot after every fourth sc, and increasing and decreasing as before, work sc across the last row to the corresponding position on opposite side. Fasten off.

First half: *Row 5:* Attach rust yarn to the center st on the first point to the left of the arm. Ch 2, work hdc as before across the next point and to the center st of the following point. Fasten off.

Second half: Attach rust yarn to the center st of the next point and work to correspond.

First half: *Row 6:* Attach orange yarn to the top of the ch-2 of the first half of the last row, work as for Row 4 to the last st of this half. Work Row 6 of the second half to correspond.

Row 7: Attach blue yarn to the first st on the arm, ch 2, and work as for Row 3. Work short rows to correspond along opposite half edge. Fasten off.

Attach brown yarn to the first st on the arm and, increasing and decreasing as before, work sc evenly all around. Join; fasten off.

Following the diagram, *below,* flatten the crocheted piece (right side up) on a padded surface, such as a carpeted floor. Using rustproof pins, carefully pin the crocheted piece into shape. Cover it with a damp terry towel; allow it to dry.

Corner: Make 4. With brown yarn, ch 28 to measure 7½ inches.

Row 1: Sc in second ch from hook, sc in each ch across; ch 1, turn.

Row 2: Sc in each sc across—27 sc. Ch 1, turn.

continued

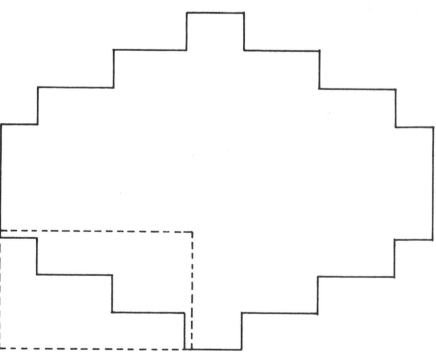

Rep Row 2 until total length is 9½ inches. End off. Following the dotted line on the diagram, slip the corner under a corner of the large piece. Pin, then sew in place. Finish all the corners in the same way to complete the rectangle.

Border: *Rnd 1:* Attach brown yarn to any corner; * 3 sc in the corner, sc evenly across to the next corner. Rep from * around. Join to first sc; ch 1, turn.

Rnds 2-4: * Sc in each sc to the center st of the next corner, 3 sc in the center st. Rep from * around. Join; ch 1, turn. At the end of Rnd 4, do not ch-1; fasten off.

Rnd 5: With blue yarn, work sc around, increasing at corners as established. Fasten off.

Rnd 6: With gold yarn, work hdc around, increasing at corners as established. Fasten off.

Rnd 7: With orange yarn, working in *back lps only*, work as for Rnd 6, making a picot after every seventh st. Fasten off.

Rnd 8: Rep Rnd 5.

Rnd 9: With purple yarn, work as for Rnd 5, making a picot after every seventh st. Fasten off.

Rnd 10: With rust yarn, rep Rnd 5. Fasten off.

Pillow: Cut two pieces of lining fabric 1 inch larger all around than the crocheted piece. With right sides together, sew the pieces together ½ inch from the edges; leave a 6-inch opening along one side. Press, and turn right side out. Stuff with fiberfill; sew opening closed. Position crocheted piece atop pillow; stitch in place.

Crocheted back: With brown yarn, make a chain (4 sts = 1 inch) the same length as the narrow edge of the pillow top.

Row 1: Sc in the second ch from the hook, sc in each ch across. Ch 3, turn.

Row 2: Dc in the second sc, dc in each sc across. Ch 1, turn.

Row 3: Sc in each dc, sc in the top of the turning-ch-3. Ch 3, turn.

Rep Rows 2 and 3 alternately until the piece is the same size as the pillow top. With top and back tog, work sc through both thicknesses along 3 edges. Insert pillow; close opening with crochet.

Indian Charcoal Pillow

Shown on page 69

Materials listed below are for a crocheted front tacked to a fabric pillow. For a crocheted pillow back, purchase three extra skeins of charcoal yarn. To crochet the back, follow directions at the end of the instructions for the Indian Cross Pillow, substituting charcoal yarn for brown yarn.

MATERIALS

For one pillow top
- Brunswick Germantown knitting worsted (3.5-ounce skeins), or a suitable substitute: 3 skeins of charcoal gray, 1 skein each of gold, rust, blue, and purple
- Size G aluminum crochet hook, or size to obtain gauge
- 2 yards of 36-inch-wide fabric for pillow lining and backing
- 2 bags of polyester fiberfill

Abbreviations: See pages 26-27.
Gauge: 4 sc = 1 inch.

INSTRUCTIONS

Center square: Beg at center with gold yarn, ch 4; join with sl st to form a ring.

Rnd 1: Ch 1, 8 sc in ring. Join with sl st to the first sc.

Rnd 2: Ch 1, 2 sc in each st around—16 sc. Join, fasten off.

Rnd 3: Attach rust yarn in any sc, ch 2, (2 hdc in next st, hdc in next st) 7 times; 2 hdc in last st. Join to the top of the ch-2 at the beg of the rnd—24 sts, counting ch-2 at the beg of the rnd as hdc.

Rnd 4: Ch 2, hdc in next 2 sts, **(ch 4, sl st in the fourth ch from the hook—picot made;** 2 hdc in next st, hdc in each of next 3 st) 5 times; 2 hdc in next st. Join to the top of the ch-2 at the beg of the rnd—30 sts—6 picots.

Rnd 5: Attach blue yarn in any st, ch 1, (sc in each of the next 14 sts, 2 sc in the next st) twice. Join to the first sc—32 sts.

Rnd 6: Ch 1, * sc in 3 sts, hdc in the next st, 2 dc in next st, **in next st make dc, trc, and dc—corner made;** 2 dc in next st, hdc in next st. Rep from * 3 more times. Join to the first sc—48 sts—4 corners.

Rnd 7: Ch 2, (hdc in each st to the center st of the next corner, in the center st make hdc, dc, and hdc) 4 times; hdc in rem sts. Join to top of ch-2—56 sts. Fasten off.

Rnd 8: Attach rust yarn in the center st of any corner, ch 1, 3 sc in same st, * make a picot, sc in next 4 sts; rep from * to the next center corner st. In the corner st work 3 sc. Rep between the *s to the next corner st; join to the first sc—64 sts. Fasten off.

Rnd 9: Attach charcoal yarn in any corner st, ch 1, 3 sc in same st, * holding picots down, sc in each st to the next corner st, 3 sc in corner st. Rep from * around; join to the first sc—72 sts.

Rnd 10: Ch 1, sc in the same st as join, * 3 sc in the next corner st, sc in each sc to the corner st, rep from * around; join to the first sc—80 sts.

Rnd 11: Ch 1, sc in the same st as join, sc in next sc, * 3 sc in next corner st, sc in each sc to the corner, rep from * around; join to the first sc—88 sts. Fasten off.

Rnd 12: Join purple yarn in any corner st, ch 1, * 3 sc in the corner st, sc in next 2 sc, **(sc in st below next sc—dropped sc made;** sk sc behind the dropped st, sc in next 3 sc) 4 times; work a dropped sc, sc in next 2 sc, rep from * around; join to the first sc—96 sts. Fasten off.

Rnd 13: Join blue yarn in any corner st, ch 1, * 3 sc in *corner* st, (sc in next 4 sc, make a picot) 5 times; sc in the next 3 sc; rep from * around; join to the first sc—104 sts. Fasten off.

Rnd 14: Join gold yarn in any corner st, ch 2, 2 hdc in same st, * holding picots down, hdc in each st to the corner, 3 hdc in the corner st, rep from * around; join to the top of the ch-2—112 sts. Fasten off.

Rnd 15: Attach rust yarn in any corner st, ch 1, 3 sc in the same st, * sc in each st to the corner, 3 sc in the next corner st, rep from * around; join to the first sc—120 sts.

Rnd 16: Ch 3, * 3 dc in the next corner st, dc in each sc to the corner, rep from * around; join to the top of the ch-3—128 sts.

Rnd 17: Ch 1, sc in the same st as join; drawing up a loop to ½ inch, sc in the st below the next dc, sk dc behind the dropped sc; * 3 sc in the corner st, (work dropped sc in st below next dc, sk dc behind dropped sc, sc in next 4 dc) 6 times; rep between * around; join to the first sc—136 sts. Fasten off.

Side: Attach charcoal yarn in the center corner st. *Row 1:* Ch 1, sc in the same st, sc in each st across to the next center corner st; ch 1, turn—35 sts.

Rows 2-12: Sc in 35 sts across the row; ch 1, turn. At the end of Row 12, do not ch 1; fasten off.

Row 13: On the right side, join purple yarn at the beg of Row 12, ch 1, sc in each sc across the row. Do not turn; fasten off.

Row 14: Attach blue yarn at the beg of Row 13, ch 1, sc in the same st and the next 4 sc, (work picot, sc in next 5 sc) 6 times; fasten off.

Row 15: Attach rust yarn at the beg of Row 14, ch 1, holding picots down, sc in each sc across the row; ch 1, turn.

Row 16: Sc in each sc across the row; fasten off.

Repeat Rows 1 through 16 along the opposite side to correspond.

Long sides: *Row 1:* With right sides up, attach purple yarn in the corner of 1 long edge, ch 1, work 63 sc evenly spaced across the row; ch 1, turn.

Row 2: Sc across row; fasten off.

Row 3: Turn, attach blue yarn in the first sc, ch 1, sc in the same st and in the next 3 sc, * work picot, work dropped sc in the st below the next sc, sk sc behind the dropped sc, sc in the next 5 sc; rep from * across, end sc in last 4 sc; fasten off.

Row 4: Attach rust yarn at beg of Row 3, ch 2, sk first sc, hdc in each sc across. Fasten off.

Row 5: With gold yarn, work triangles as follows: Join yarn in the top of the ch-2 at the beg of Row 4, ch 1, sc in the same st, sc in the next 6 sc; ch 1, turn. Sk the first sc, sc in the next 6 sc; ch 1, turn; * sk the first sc, sc across the row; ch 1, turn; rep from *s until all sts have been worked; fasten off.

Join yarn in *next* sc on Row 4 and work another triangle as explained above; fasten off. Continue across the row, working triangles—9 triangles made.

Row 6: Attach rust yarn at the beg of the first triangle on Row 5, ch 1, sc in the same st, * work 4 sc evenly spaced to the top of the triangle, work picot, work 4 sc down the side of the triangle; work dec over next 2 sc as follows: (work in the last row of the first triangle and the first row of the next triangle); draw up a lp in each of these 2 sts, yo, draw through 3 lps on the hook; rep bet * across the row; end with 5 sc down side of the last triangle. Fasten off.

Row 7: Attach blue yarn in the first sc at the beg of Row 6, ch 3, **(yo, draw up loop in next sc, yo, draw through 2 lps on hook) 2 times; yo, draw through 3 lps on hook, ch 1 for eye—first cluster (cl) made;** sc in next 2 sc, * sc in the top of the triangle (behind picot), sc in next 2 sc, **work a dc-cl over next 5 sc as follows: (yo, draw up a lp in next sc, yo, draw through 2 lps on hook) 5 times, yo, draw through 6 lps on hook, ch 1 for eye of cl,** sc in next 2 sc; rep from * across the row, ending with dc-cl over the last 3 sc. Fasten off.

Row 8: Attach purple yarn in the top of the ch-3 at the beg of Row 7, ch 2, * work 2 hdc in the eye of the next cl, sc in next 5 sc, rep from * across; end with 2 hdc in the top of the last cl—66 sts across the row, counting the beg ch-2 as 1 st. Fasten off.

Row 9: Attach rust yarn in the top of the ch-2 at the beg of Row 8, ch 1, sc in each st across the row; ch 2, turn.

Row 10: Sk first sc, work hdc in each sc across the row; ch 1, turn.

Row 11: Sc in the first 4 sts, work picot, * sc in 8 sts, work picot, rep from * across row; end with sc in last 5 sc and in the top of the turning-ch; ch 2, turn.

Row 12: Sk first sc, hdc in each sc across row; ch 1, turn.

Row 13: Sc in each st across the row and in the top of the turning-ch; ch 2, turn.

Row 14: Rep Row 12; do not ch-1 at the end of the row; fasten off.

Row 15: Attach charcoal yarn in the first sc, ch 1, sc in each st across the row, ch 1, turn.

Rows 16-26: Sc in each sc across the row; ch 1, turn. Do not ch-1 at the end of Row 26; fasten off.

Row 27: Attach rust yarn in sc, ch 1, sc in each sc across the row; ch 2, turn.

Row 28: Sk first sc, hdc in each sc across the row; fasten off.

Row 29: With right side facing, attach blue yarn, ch 1, sc in the first 3 sts, * work picot, sc in the next 6 sc; rep from * across the row; end with sc in the last 3 sc. Fasten off.

Row 30: Attach purple yarn at the beg of Row 29, ch 2, hdc in each sc across the row; fasten off.

Rep Rows 1-30 on the opposite side of the pillow top to correspond.

Finishing rnd: This rnd works around the whole pillow top. Work in sts when they are available; otherwise work evenly spaced in the edge of the rows.

Attach rust yarn in any corner st, in the same st work (sc, picot, sc); * work sc in the next 3 sts, work picot; rep from the * to the next corner st; in the corner st work (sc, picot, sc). Continue as established around the pillow top.

Finishing: Cut two pieces of fabric 1 inch larger all around than the crocheted piece. With the right sides facing, sew the pieces together ½ inch from the raw edges, leaving a 6-inch-long opening in one side. Press and turn right side out. Stuff firmly with polyester fiberfill; sew the opening closed. With sewing thread, tack the crochet piece to the pillow form.

ACKNOWLEDGMENTS

We wish to express our appreciation to the designers, photographers, and others who contributed to this book. When more than one project appears on a page, the acknowledgment specifically cites the project with the page number. A page number alone indicates one designer or source has contributed all of the project material listed for that page.

Our special thanks to the following designers who contributed crochet projects to this book.

Ginger Basset—66-67
Gary Boling—65, scrap yarn coverlet
Lezli Harris—16, filet edging with scallops
Gail Kinkead—6-7; 16, filet edging; 30, pineapple doily; cover, pineapple doily
Susan Morrow—68-69
Mary Lynn Patrick—53, man's cardigan
Sara Jane Treinen—table runner, cover; 31

For their cooperation and courtesy, we extend a special thanks to the following sources for designs and projects.

Talon-American Thread
—65, shell afghan
High Ridge Park
Stamford, CT 06905
The Bucilla Company
—48-49
150 Meadowlands Parkway
P. O. Box 1534
Secaucus, NJ 07094
Coats & Clark, Inc.
—4-5; 7-8; 50-51; 52;
53, popcorn stitch cardigan
72 Cummings Point Road
Stamford, CT 06902
D.M.C. Corporation
—18
197 Trumbull Street
Elizabeth, NJ 07206
King Features Patterns
—32-33
Box 143
New York, NY 10011
F.D.R. Hyde Park Museum
—34-35
249 Albany Post Road
Hyde Park, NY 12538
Reynolds Yarn Company
—46-47
1170 Broadway, Room 912
New York, NY 10001
William Unger and Company, Inc.
—62-63
230 Fifth Avenue
New York, NY 10001

We also are pleased to acknowledge the following photographers, whose talents and technical skills contributed much to this book.

Mike Dieter—cover, 31
de Gennaro Studios—53, man's cardigan
Hedrich-Blessing—4-5; 7, five-sided pineapple doily; 19; 46-47; 50
Hopkins Associates—6; 7, centerpiece doily with violets; 16-17; 64; 68-69
Thomas Hooper—18; 28; 34-35; 38; 62-63; 65, scrap afghan
Bradley Olman—32-33; 52; 53, popcorn stitch cardigan
Perry Struse—48-49; 51; 67

Have BETTER HOMES AND GARDENS® magazine delivered to your door. For information, write to: MR. ROBERT AUSTIN, P.O. BOX 4536, DES MOINES, IA 50336.